Costumes with Character

Amy Puetz

To my sisters, Sarah and Marissa.
Thank you both for all the fun times we had playing as children,
such as all the trips we made west in our canopy bed,
the ship we made in front of the kitchen door, and the times
we played like we were southern belles during the Civil War.
What happy memories!

Copyright 2010 by Amy Puetz
All Rights Reserved.
No part of this book may be reproduced in any form or by any electronic or mechanical means including information storage and retrieval systems, without permission in writing from the author. The only exception is by a reviewer, who may quote short excerpts in a review.

Published by Golden Prairie Press
P.O. Box 429, Wright, WY 82732
www.AmyPuetz.com

Cover & Layout Design - Amy Puetz
Models - Marissa, Sarah, Marissa, Mary Evelyn, Elizabeth, and Amy
Photography of costumes - Amy Puetz and Phyllis Puetz
Images - Library of Congress, *Historic Dress in America*, out of print books

VELCRO® is a registered trademark of Velcro Industries B. V.
Wonder-Under is a registered trademark of Pellon.

Works Cited
Cockrum, William Monroe, *Pioneer History of Indiana*, 1907
Fales, Jane, *Dressmaking*, 1917
Houghton, Eliza P. Donner, *The Expedition of the Donner Party and its Tragic Fate*, 1920
Marble, Annie Russell, *The Women Who Came in the Mayflower*, 1920
McClellan, Elizabeth, *Historic Dress in America*, (volume 1) 1904 and (volume 2) 1910
McKnight, William James, *A Pioneer Outline History of Northwestern Pennsylvania*, 1905
Kittredge, Mabel Hyde, *Practical Homemaking; a Textbook for Young Housekeepers*, 1915
Williams, Walter, *The State of Missouri*, 1905
Etiquette for Americans, 1898
Godey's Magazine, 1894 and 1895
Household Words, 1885
The Delineator Magazine, 1902, 1903, and 1905
The London and Paris Ladies' Magazine of Fashion, 1881

ISBN: 978-0-9825199-4-3
LCCN: 2010910479

Library of Congress Cataloging-in-Publication Data

Includes index.
I. 1. Fashion—History. 2. Clothing and dress—History. 3. Costume—History. 4. Costume—United States. 5. Clothing and dress—United States.
II. Title

Contents

Foreword..v
Introduction..vi
Dress..1
Colonial (Pilgrim & Puritan 1620 - 1700)..................................3
Quaker (1681 - 1860)..11
American Revolution (1775 - 1783)...15
Young Republic (1800 - 1820)...23
Romantic Era (1820 - 1848)..27
Pioneer (1800s)..34
Civil War (1861 - 1865)..39
Sailor (1865 - 1905)..46
Victorian 1880s..52
Victorian 1890s..58
Turn of the Century (1900 - 1910)..65
Tea Party...70
Index...72
Bibliography..72

Let us run the risk of wearing out
rather than rusting out.
-Theodore Roosevelt

Make today right and tomorrow
may be right of itself.
-Sarah Hale

The smallest things are as absolutely
necessary as the great things.
-Mary Slessor

As the daylight can be seen through very small holes
so little things will illustrate a person's character.
Indeed, character consists in little acts, well and honorably performed.
-Smiles

Stay is a charming word in
a friend's vocabulary.
-Louisa May Alcott

If we had not winter, the spring would not be
so pleasant. If we did not sometimes taste
adversity, prosperity would not be so welcome.
-Anne Bradstreet

The art of self-government is
indispensable to woman's felicity.
-Sarah Hale

Foreword
by Jennie Chancey

"Mom, do we have a parasol?" I asked, digging through the upstairs hall trunk. "Well," my mother replied, "I know we *used* to have an old Japanese parasol that belonged to your grandmother, but we can always make a parasol from an umbrella!" An hour later, I was promenading in the back yard with my lacey 'brella and feeling like a queen.

While growing up and homeschooling, our family loved to "play dress-up" as we studied historical events. We also got together with fellow homeschoolers to put on history plays, and it was always interesting to see what kinds of costumes everyone came up with. For medieval times, we cooked a period feast and dressed in costumes we cobbled together from the dress-up trunk. When we read about the pioneers, I made a bonnet and created a "kind of" accurate outfit from a dress and an apron. When we hit the War Between the States, I pined for a hoopskirt but made do with my grandmother's old crinoline petticoats from the 1950s. Creating costumes from what we had on hand and making fun accessories to go with them was the icing on the cake as we studied timelines, names, and places.

Many mothers dread the thought of sewing something from scratch, especially since commercial patterns are often very time-consuming and daunting for the inexperienced seamstress. Yet there is something extra special about being able to "live" history as we study it, and girls especially find it thrilling to dress like Pilgrims or pioneers. Often it just isn't possible to attempt costuming because of the costs and time involved.

That is all about to change. You hold in your hands the answer to these concerns, and I am absolutely thrilled to promote Amy Puetz's wonderful book, *Costumes with Character*. From one beautifully detailed page to the next, you will see how simple it is to take a basic dress and turn it into eleven different costumes, spanning from the 17th century to the early 1900s. You will be amazed at how little effort it takes to go from one era to the next with a change of collar and cuffs or the addition of a bonnet! Amy's clear instructions and illustrations make all of the sewing steps easy to follow, and her historical quotations, and Q&A in each section will spark further interest in each time period.

It *is* possible to create wonderful costumes to portray historical events without emptying your pocketbook or losing your mind over complicated directions. If you are looking for a fun way to introduce daughters to sewing, this book is also a super jumping-off point. Whatever the event, I believe you'll find *Costumes with Character* a tremendous creativity-booster. Thank you, Amy, for this historical treat!

Jennie Chancey
Homeschooling mom and owner of Sense & Sensibility Patterns

Introduction
Adjusting the patterns

I hope you enjoy this book as much as I enjoyed writing it. History is so exciting to study, and what better way to learn about it than by dressing up in historical outfits from different time periods?

The patterns in this book are for ages sixteen and up. Below is a chart for making the patterns to fit smaller girls. You may want to make some of the patterns, such as the collars and hats the original size so they fit for many years. The cuffs should be measured according to the size of the wrist and arm. The other patterns, such as the aprons and vests, should probably be made to fit.

For example, let us say you want to make the apron in the Colonial chapter and your child is nine years old. The length will be determined by how tall she is and how much fabric you have. The width of the apron is 24", so we need to reduce the size by 12%. The equation would look like this:

24"x12% = 2.88"
24" - 2.88" = 21.12" round the number to 21"

Therefore, make the apron 21" wide rather than the 24" in the patterns. Use the equation above and the measurement chart below as a guide to reducing the size of the patterns.

Measurement Chart

Approx. Age	4-5	6-7	8-11	12-14	16 and up
Chest	26	28	30	32	34
Waist	22	23	24	26	28
Reduce the size of the patterns by	24%	18%	12%	6%	no reduction.

Several patterns call for paper-backed fusible web my favorite kind is Wonder-Under.

You can also make a simple dress for a doll, then make the costumes in this book to fit the doll. Then the doll and girl can have matching outfits.

Each chapter begins with a short overview of the history of the era and the clothing that was worn. I begin by sharing about the era and my writing is indented and in a smaller text. The historical notes from period sources are in a larger font. For a more in-depth study of historical costumes see the bibliography in the back. This list shares my favorite historical costumes and the ones I used to help me with write book.

I sincerely hope you have a great time making the clothes in this book and enjoy pretending to live during the eras covered in this book. God bless you all.

Pilgrim on a journey,
Amy Puetz

The Dress
Finding the Perfect Frock

My fingers ran along the hem of the most beautiful white dress I had ever seen. Voices in the background brought me back from my rapture as I heard my grandma say something about purchasing the dress at a garage sale with the plan of cutting off the bodice to make a skirt from the bottom part of the dress. "But I never got around to it, so the girls can have it as a play dress." Had I heard correctly? Grandma said my sisters and I could have this beautiful dress! It was too wonderful to be true.

When I was a little girl we went to visit my grandma and while rummaging around in her back closet she found this magnificent frock. The dress was made from wide seersucker fabric and had lace trim along the cuffs and skirt ruffle. Although the sleeves did not have the puff that Anne Shirley from Green Gables would have wanted, it did have a slight poof to them and the collar was made of a little ruffle. Even though it was much too large for my sisters and me, we absolutely loved it. From that time on the white dress became our favorite garment for play.

My sisters and me. Sarah in the white dress, Marissa (middle), and Amy (right).

With our vivid imaginations we could transform the dress to almost any time period. One day it would be the perfect dinner gown for a party set in the 1940s; the next day it would be a fashionable dress of a western woman. At the waist we would pull up the long skirt and pin it, which gave the look of a bustle and the extra skirt would cascade down the back in a long train. This was perfect for a Victorian tea party and other social gatherings that occupy girls at play.

From that very early age I began my love for historical costumes. My sisters and I enjoyed historical movies such as *Anne of Green Gables, The Robe*, and *How the West was Won*. Obviously our mother wasn't going to make us a new costume each time we found a good historical movie, so we learned to improvise. In our large box of play clothes—hand-me downs from our mother and adult clothes from garage sales—we would put different skirts and blouses together to form different looks. From the same garments we created costumes for every time period from the Biblical era to the 1950s. With the addition of a few essentials such as sunbonnets, hats, gloves, and belts we were able to put together a variety of outfits.

In this book I share the simple idea of taking one dress and transforming it into styles from different eras. *Costumes with Character* utilizes the concept of one dress costuming. With the simple addition of cuffs, collars, belts, aprons, etc., one gown can easily be altered to reflect the fashion of different time periods. This book is much more sophisticated than my childish attempts to make the white dress change from one frock to another. In my imagination there is no doubt that the white dress looked exactly as I wished, but any other observer would probably have seen it differently! I hope you enjoy this book and discover the world of historical costuming.

Amy in the white dress and Marissa

2   Costumes with Character

A simple dress can be used for so many time periods that it is an essential for any girl or young lady who loves historical costumes. When the dress is completed, the costumes are half done! Then add the accessories for each costume.

There are different ways to get a dress that will work. It may be sewn using a pattern (like the blue dress at right and the pink dress below), or you may make over a dress you already have (like the green dress below). The green dress was a size 12 lady's dress that has been altered to fit an eight-year-old girl.

If you find or make a solid color dress, then the accessories may be of a printed fabric (or vice versa if the dress has a pattern on it). Instead of a dress you may use a blouse (white is always a good choice) and a long skirt for some of the time periods. Garage sales and second hand stores often have dresses that work for the simple dress that is just calling for accessories.

If using a pattern it should be a basic and simple dress. The easiest way to get a dress for a child is to find an adult dress and take up the side seams, hem, and sleeves. The dress and sleeves can be made with deep hems to be let out as the girl grows. Let your imagination soar!

Things to look for in a pattern:
- ~ no collar
- ~ simple sleeves
- ~ full skirt
- ~ long skirt

Visit www.AmyPuetz.com/Costumes.html for pattern sources.

You may also make a simple dress for a doll and then use the patterns in this book to make accessories for her as well!

Colonial
Pilgrim and Puritan
1620-1700

Bravely they came, and heroically they stayed. What courage it must have taken for the women and girls who came to America on the *Mayflower*. No doubt the stories of other attempts at colonization crossed their minds. Did they think about the lost colony at Roanoke and the struggling colony at Jamestown? Possibly, but they knew setting up a home in America was God's will and they bravely followed their husbands and fathers to the New World.

There were approximately eighteen married women and ten girls on the *Mayflower*. Sadly only four women survived the first winter. They were: Mary Brewster, Susan Winslow, Elizabeth Hopkins, and Ellen Billington. In *Of Plymouth Plantation,* Ellen More is the only girl whom William Bradford mentions as dying the first winter. The other girls of the *Mayflower* went on to marry and many of them have numerous decedents. Among the most famous of these Pilgrim girls were: Priscilla Mullins, Mary Chilton, Elizabeth Tillie, and Constanta (Constance) Hopkins. The first three in the list lost their parents during the general sickness of the initial winter. It is possible that they lived with William and Mary Brewster until they married.

These women and girls were real people. They had joy and sorrow, enjoyed pretty things, learned to do without, and most of all they did daily mundane activities just as we do. Their very lives depended on their ability to provide food, clothing, and shelter to their families. When thinking of historical women, try to remember that they were very much like us. Their dress and manner of speaking were different, but underneath humans are basically the same down through the ages.

The Pilgrims going to church

In *The Women Who Came in the Mayflower,* author Annie Russell Marble describes how the Pilgrims dressed.

The first Thanksgiving

What did these Pilgrim women wear? The manifest answer is, what they had in stock. No more absurd idea was ever invented than the picture of these Pilgrims "in uniform," gray gowns with dainty white collars and cuffs, with stiff caps and dark capes. They wore the typical garments of the period for men and women in England. There is no evidence that they adopted, to any extent, Dutch dress, for they were proud of their English birth; they left Holland partly for fear that their young people might be educated or enticed away from English standards of conduct.

Costumes with Character

The women wore full skirts of silk of varied colors, long, pointed stomachers—often with a bright tone, sometimes puffed or slashed sleeves, and lace collars or "whisks" resting upon the shoulders. [Whisk is a collar which covers the neck and shoulders, usually made of muslin trimmed with lace.] Sometimes the gowns were plaited or silk-laced; they often opened in front showing petticoats that were quilted or embroidered in brighter colors. Broadcloth gowns of russet tones were worn by those who could not afford silks and satins; sometimes women wore doublets [a garment usually made of two thicknesses, thus its name] and jerkins [another name for jacket or doublet] of black and browns. Velvet and quilted hoods

Landing of the Pilgrims

of all colors and sometimes caps, flat on the head and meeting below the chin with fullness, are shown in existent portraits of English women and early colonists.

Among relics that are dated back to this early period are the slippers belonging to Mistress Susanna White Winslow, narrow, pointed, with lace trimmings, and an embroidered lace cap that has been assigned to Rose Standish. Sometimes the high ruffs were worn above the shoulders instead of "whisks." The children were dressed like miniature men and women; often the girls wore aprons, as did the women on occasions; these were narrow and edged with lace. "Petty coats" are mentioned in wills among the garments of the women. We would not assume that in 1621-2 all the women in Plymouth colony wore silken or even homespun clothes of prevailing English fashion. Many of these that are mentioned in inventories and retained as heirlooms, with rich laces and embroideries, were brought later from England; probably Winslow, Allerton, and even Standish brought back such gifts to the women when they made their trips to England in 1624 and later. If the Pilgrim women had laces and embroideries of gold they probably hoarded them as precious heirlooms during those early years of want, for they were too sensible to wear and to waste them. As prosperity came, however, and new elements entered the colony they were, doubtless, affected by the law of the General Court, in 1634, which forbade further acquisition of laces, threads of silver and gold, needle-work caps, bands and rails, and silver girdles and belts. This law was enacted not by the Pilgrims of Plymouth, but by the Puritans of Massachusetts Bay Colony.

> The Pilgrims were followed to the New World by the Puritans who settled in the Massachusetts Bay area in 1630. While the Pilgrims were Separatists (who wanted to separate from the Church of England), the Puritans tried to "purify" the church from within. Reforms were not easy and many Puritans looked to America as a place where they could enjoy religious freedom. The Puritans were very strict in their dress, in fact they were even called Roundheads because the men's hair was worn in a plain round style.
>
> Below are some interesting facts about Puritan dress from *Historic Dress of America* by Elizabeth McClellan.

Margaret Winthrop, [the wife of Governor John Winthrop] in a letter to England written from Massachusetts, gives a note of daily wear: 'I must of a necessity make me a gown to wear every day and would have one bought me of good strong black stuff and Mr. Smith to make it of the civilest fashion now in use. If my sister Downing would please to give him some directions about it, he would make it the better.' Slight as is this note, it proves that Dame Winthrop was not indifferent to the prevailing fashions. The familiar portrait of Governor Winthrop in a ruff and long hair indicates that he had not adopted the dress of the strict Puritans. Unfortunately, no portrait of his wife has been handed down to posterity, and we are left to conjecture that the dress of 'good strong black stuff' to 'wear every day' was made of Durant [a woolen fabric], something after the fashion of the picture at right.

Puritan couple

The couple below shows the dress of the Puritans. His suit of black cloth is of the same cut as a Cavalier's only without trimmings. Stockings or hose of dark gray or green wool fastened to the breeches by points of black ribbons. The collar and cuffs are of white Holland linen. The hat of black felt finished with a narrow band of ribbon and a small silver buckle. The cloak is of black cloth. The lady's gown is either purple or gray, or perhaps brown; for outdoor wear it is turned under and looped back showing petticoats of homespun or linsey-woolsey. The

Puritan couple

apron is of white Holland linen. A collar goes around the neck of the gown and white linen cuffs are turned back over the sleeves. The hood is made of dark colored silk and lined with soft silk or fur to match the muff. Stout shoes with wooden heels and woolen stockings completed the costumes. The hair is drawn back under a white linen cap and an apron covers the front of the dress. This was the ordinary dress of a Puritan gentlewomen from 1620-1640.

The majority of the Puritans were very much in earnest on the subject of reform in dress, and it has been said they expressed their piety not only in the choice of somber hues and simplicity of cut, but even worked into the garments religious sayings and quotations from the Holy Writ. This fashionable custom in England is also mentioned by Ben Jonson, 'The linen of men and women was either so worked as to resemble lace or was ornamented by the needle into representations of fruit and flowers, passages of history, etc.'

Recommended Resources

The Courtship of Miles Standish by Henry Wadsworth Longfellow
Almost Home, a Story Based on the Life of the Mayflower's Mary Chilton by Wendy Lawton
The Light and the Glory by Peter Marshall & David Manuel
Of Plymouth Plantation by William Bradford
If You Sailed on the Mayflower by Ann McGovern
Three Young Pilgrims by Cheryl Harness
Sweet Land of Liberty by Charles C. Coffin

Find recommended resources for the other eras at www.AmyPuetz.com/CWCresources.html

Costumes with Character

They cherished a great hope and inward zeal of laying good foundations, or at least of making some way towards it, for the propagation and advance of the gospel of the kingdom of Christ in the remote parts of the world. -William Bradford, giving one of the reasons they came to the New World

She has a strange sweetness in her mind, and singular purity in her affections; is most just and conscientious in all her conduct; and you could not persuade her to do any thing wrong or sinful, if you would give her all the world, lest she should offend this Great Being.
-Jonathan Edwards on Sarah Pierrepont's character four years before she became his wife

Pilgrim Dress *Puritan Dress*

For we must consider that we shall be as a "City upon a Hill." The eyes of all people are upon us; so that if we shall deal falsely with our God in this work, we have undertaken and so cause Him to withdraw His present help from us, we shall open the mouths of enemies to speak evil of the ways of God and all professors for God's sake; we shall shame the faces of many of God's worthy servants, and cause their prayers to be turned into curses upon us till we be consumed out of the good land whither we are going. -John Winthrop in a sermon titled "A Model of Charity"

The Pilgrim Dress

Collar

> White fabric
> Hook and eye
> Iron-on interfacing for midweight fabric
> Paper-backed fusible web (optional)

Instructions
1. Use the collar pattern on page 10 as a guide to cut out fabric.
2. Iron interfacing on the wrong side of one of the collar pieces.
3. Sew with right sides together using ¼" seam and leaving 2½" opening to turn through (FIG. 1). Notch around neck and clip corners.
4. Turn the collar right side out and press.
5. Iron a small piece of the fusible web on the opening in the back, let cool, then tear the paper off and iron again. This will close up the opening in the back, or you may hand stitch the opening closed.
6. Hand stitch hook and eye (FIG. 2).

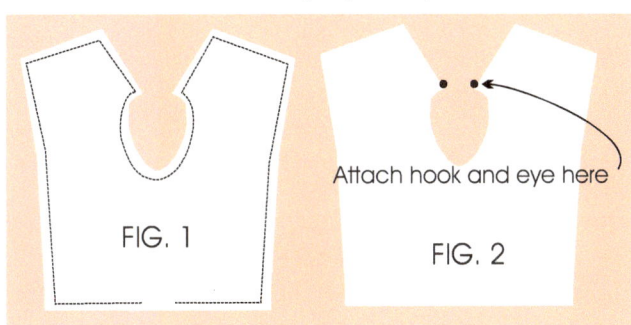

7. To wear, place collar over dress. It may be safety pinned to the dress.

Cuffs

> ¼" elastic
> White fabric
> Iron-on interfacing for midweight fabric

Instructions (make two)
1. Use the patterns on page 10 as a guide to cut out fabric for cuffs and casing. Cut out interfacing just a little smaller than the cuff piece.
2. Iron interfacing on the wrong side of one of the cuff pieces.
3. Place right sides of the cuffs together and stitch around three sides, using ¼" seam and leaving the bottom open. Clip corners, turn right side out, and press.
4. Fold and press ¼" to inside of casing piece lengthwise on both sides so when sewed there will be a finished edge. Fold wrong side together lengthwise and press. Crease one short end ¼".
5. Place open bottom end of cuff in the casing. Top stitch the casing to the cuff piece through all thickness so you have a finished top stitch on both sides (FIG. 3).

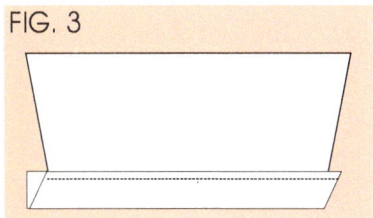

6. Thread elastic (the size of the wrist plus ½" for seam allowance) through casing. Sew the elastic ends together. Close the opening of the casing by putting the raw edge into the creased edge (FIG. 4) and top stitch.

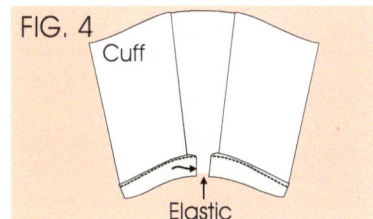

7. To wear, tuck the casing part under the sleeve so only the cuff is visible. It may be secured with safety pins to keep in place.

Hat

> White fabric
> Two - 25"x¼" white ribbon
> Iron-on interfacing for midweight fabric
> Fabric that matches the dress
> Paper-backed fusible web

Instructions
1. Use the hat patterns on page 10 as a guide to cutting out the fabric. Iron interfacing on the wrong side of the white fabric.
2. Place right sides together. Pin ribbon 3¾" from the top edge. Sew together using a ½" seam allowance. Leaving a 2" opening in the back for turning (FIG. 5).

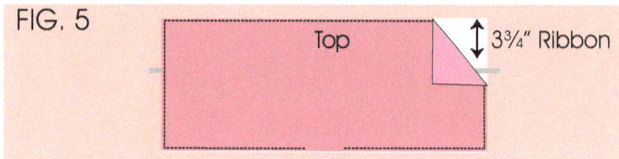

FIG. 5

3. Notch corners, turn right side out and press.
4. Iron a small piece of the fusible web on the opening in the back, let cool, then tear the paper off and iron again. This will close up the opening in the back, or you may hand stitch the opening closed.
5. Fold the pink fabric (or whatever color you are using) together at the ribbons (FIG. 6) and press.

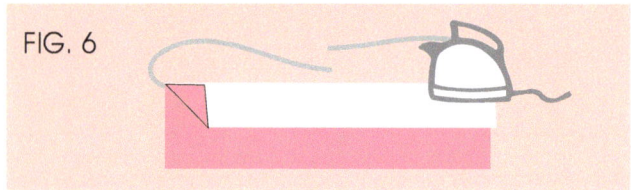

FIG. 6

6. To wear, place on head and tie under the chin with ribbons.

Apron
 White fabric

Instructions
1. Use the apron patterns on page 10 as a guide to cut out the fabric.
2. Hem three sides to give a finished edge and gather top of apron (FIG. 7).

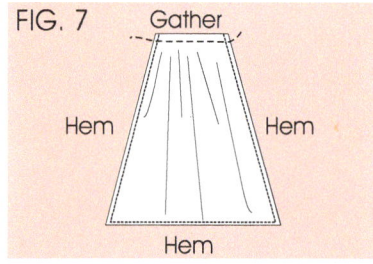

3. Fold waistband on all four sides ½" down on wrong side and press (FIG. 8). Fold in half lengthwise, wrong sides together, and press.

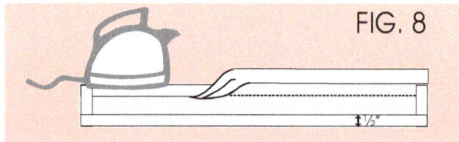

4. Mark the center of both the apron and waistband with pins.
5. Line up the center of both pieces, using the pins as guides. Top stitch waistband to apron over gathered edge of apron and continue top stitching the remainder of the waistband.

The Puritan Dress

Collar
 White fabric
 Iron-on interfacing for midweight fabric
 Hook and eye
 Paper-backed fusible web (optional)

Instructions
1. Use the collar patterns on page 10 as a guide to cut out the fabric.
2. Iron interfacing on the wrong side of one of the collar pieces.
3. Sew with right sides together, using ¼" seam and leaving 2½" opening to turn through (FIG. 9). Notch around neck and clip corners.
4. Turn the collar right side out and press.
5. Iron a small piece of the fusible web on the opening in the back, let cool, then tear the paper off and iron again. This will close up the opening in the back, or you may hand stitch the opening closed.
6. Hand stitch hook and eye (FIG. 10).

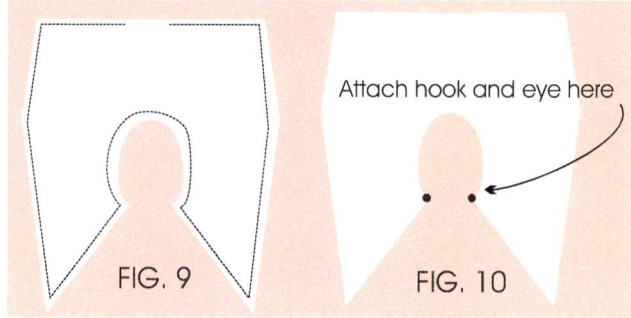

7. To wear, place collar over dress. It may be safety pinned to the dress.

Lawn Cap
 White fabric
 Two - 20"x¼" white ribbon
 Lace (optional)

Instructions
1. Cut out the lawn cap crown and lawn cap back. A 2"x80" piece of white fabric for the ruffle or 1" lace may be used. Patterns are on page 10.
2. If using lace, skip step 2. Fold the ruffle piece in half and press. Gather the ruffle until it is the same size as the cap.
3. Place the crown pieces right sides together and pin the raw edge of the ruffle or lace in between the

two crown pieces along the angled edge and the two short ends. Leave a tail of ruffle on each end. Place ribbons for the ties on the corners. Pin all the layers together. Sew three sides together using, ½" seam allowance (FIG. 11). Turn right side out and press.

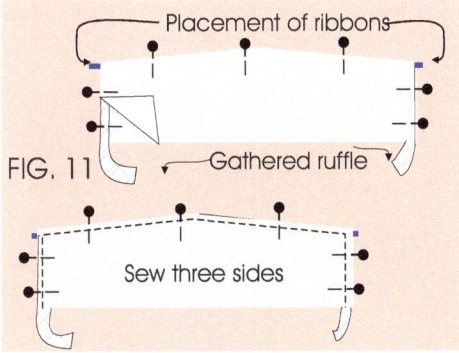

4. Take the cap back and fold and press the straight edge ¼" and then another ¼".

5. On the cap crown designate the side that the ribbons came out on as the wrong side. With right sides together, place the raw edge of the cap crown to the cap back. Sew together, using ½" seam allowance. Top stitch the remaining ruffle to the back of the cap (FIG. 12).

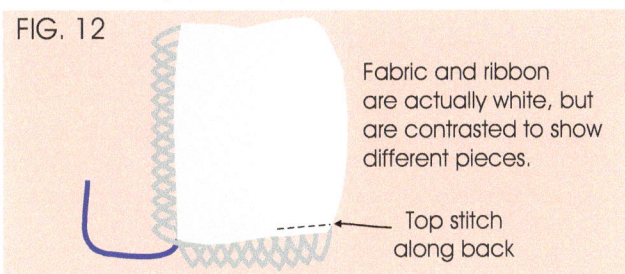

6. To wear, place on head and tie under chin with ribbons.

Cuffs and Apron - same as the Pilgrim dress.

Advice to a Son
by Anne Bradstreet

~ Sweet words are like honey, a little may refresh, but too much gluts the stomach.
~ Authority without wisdom is like a heavy axe without an edge, fitter to bruise than polish.
~ Wickedness comes to its height by degrees. He that dares say of a little sin, "Is it not a little one?" will ere long say of a greater "Tush, God regards it not!"

Questions about the Pilgrims & Puritans

Answers are below.
1. What was the name of the Pilgrim's ship?
2. What was the name of the document that the Pilgrims signed before leaving their ship?
3. Name the religious group of the Pilgrims. (A) Puritans (B) Separatist (C) Church of England
4. Name the first governor of Plymouth Plantation.
5. Who was the lady in Longfellow's *The Courtship of Miles Standish*?
6. Name the Indian who was so helpful to the Pilgrims.
7. Of the original 101 Pilgrims, how many died the first winter? (A) 8 (B) 47 (C) 87
8. Why did the Pilgrims celebrate the first Thanksgiving?
9. The Puritans were trying to purify what religious institution?
10. The Puritans came from this country. What was it?
11. Name the man who led nearly 1,000 people to the New World and began several settlements in the Massachusetts Bay. He was also the governor of the Bay Colony.
12. What famous college was started by the Puritans in 1636 to train ministers? It was the first college started in New England.
13. What was the name of the Puritan minister who preached "Sinners in the Hands of an Angry God"?
14. There was a spiritual revival that began in 1740 and lasted until 1742. What was the revival called?
15. Which father and son were well known Puritan ministers in Boston?

1. The *Mayflower* 2. The Mayflower Compact 3. Separatist 4. William Bradford 5. Priscilla Mullins 6. Squanto 7. 47 8. The Pilgrims celebrated a time of thanking God for preserving them. They asked the Indians to join them. 9. The Church of England 10. England 11. John Winthrop 12. Harvard 13. Jonathan Edwards 14. The Great Awakening 15. Increase and Cotton Mather

Pilgrim & Puritan Patterns

Pilgrim Hat
21"x10"
cut 2 - one of white and
one the same color as the dress

Pilgrim Collar
cut 2
each square
equals 1 inch

Place on fold

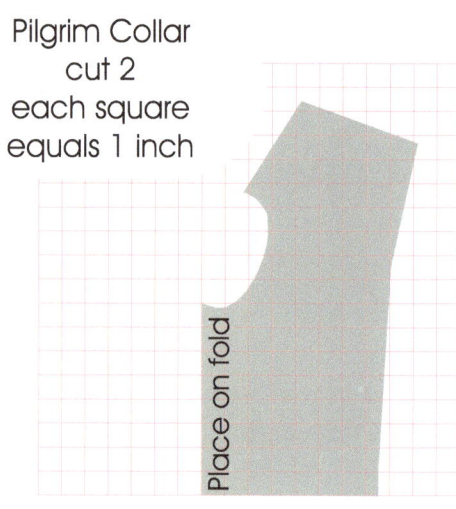

Cuff
cut 4
Top 11" or 2" wider than bottom
4"
Bottom 9" or the width around the wrist

Cuff Elastic Casing
2"x9" or the width around the wrist
cut 2

Apron Waistband
60"x4½"
cut 1

This may be pieced if needed

Apron
24"x32" (or desired length)
cut 1

Puritan Lawn Cap Crown
cut 2
fold 7"
6"
10 ½"

Puritan Collar
cut 2
fold

Lawn Cap Back
8½"x7"
cut 1

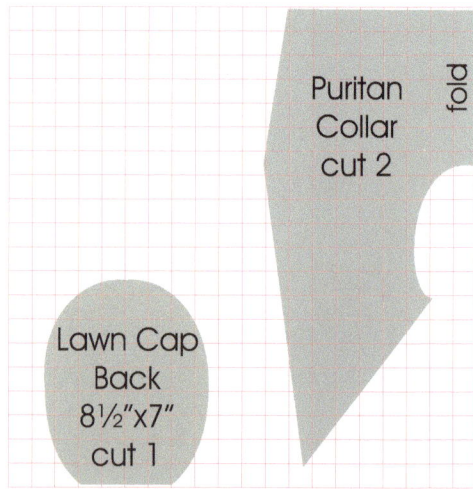

Quaker

1681-1860

The colony of Pennsylvania was started by a Quaker gentleman named William Penn. Since the Quakers suffered harsh persecution in England they willingly faced the dangerous of the New World to enjoy religious freedom. Sometimes Quakers are referred to as the Society of Friends and they called each other Friends. Many of the practices of the Quakers seemed strange to other colonists. The Quakers did not believe in removing their hats, they said *thee* and *thou* instead of *you* and *your*. The first Quaker colonists dressed fashionably but as time went by they began to adopt a strict form of dress.

Ladies and girls of all ages wore what has come down through the ages as "the Quaker bonnet." This bonnet was usually white and might be made of silk or sheer lawn. Some of these bonnets looked like a sunbonnet of the pioneer era and others looks like hats.

In *Historic Dress in America* author Elizabeth McClellan describes the Quakers mode of dress.

Quaker Dress in 1680s

The picture at right shows a Quaker gentleman in a suit of dark brown or plum-colored cloth cut according to the English fashion at the end of Charles II's reign. The full shirt-sleeves hang in ruffles over the hand and the neck-cloth, though of the fashionable style and of the finest linen, is untrimmed. The hat is of the shape seen in the portraits of the time. The absence of feathers and lace was the only distinction of Quaker dress before 1700. The hair was occasionally powdered and wigs were not uncommon, but the hair was usually worn in natural locks parted in the middle and hanging to the shoulders.

This picture (above) shows the typical dress of a Quaker lady of 1680-1700 with a gown of some soft colored silk with fine white kerchief and under-sleeves. The long full apron is also of silk, probably a dull green. The early Quaker colonists loved green! Under the black silk hood for outdoor wear a ruffled cap of sheer lawn is worn. The hair is parted in front and arranged in a coil at the back.

In the early part of the 1800s the Quakers were more rigid in their regulations with regard to dress. In the *Autobiography of Mary Howitt* she describes the austerely plain costumes of a little

The Landing of William Penn by Jean Leon Gerome Ferris
A variety of costumes are represented in this painting

Quaker Dress 1800s

Quaker Dress 1860

Quaker girl in 1809, 'How well I remember the garments that were made for us. Our little brown cloth pelisses [a long coat like garment usually made to fit the figure], cut plain and straight, without plait or fold in them, hooked and eyed down the front so as to avoid buttons, which were regarded by our parents as trimmings, yet fastened at the waist, with a cord. Little drab beaver bonnets furnished us by the Friends' hatter of Stafford, James Nixon, who had bonnet forms made purposely for our little ultra-plain bonnets. They were without a scrap of ribbon or cord, except the strings, which were a necessity, and these were fastened inside. Our frocks were, as usual, of the plainest and most homely fabric and make.' Nothing could be more sad and doleful than the garb at left, copied from the woodcut in the book.

The bonnets worn by Quaker ladies were decidedly distinctive. A picture of one may be seen in the above insert at right. The slight changes in Quaker fashion are exemplified in the interesting costume pictured at right, which resembles with absolute fidelity the dress of Elizabeth Fry in the portrait by Richmond painted in 1824, although it was worn by a Quaker lady named Mrs. Johnson of Philadelphia about 1860.

Recommended Resources

Daughters of Destiny by Noelle Goforth. Read the chapters about Dolley Madison, Lydia Darrah, and Betsy Ross

Light and the Glory by Peter Marshall & David Manuel

Sweet Land of Liberty by Charles C. Coffin

Movie - *Friendly Persuasion* (1956) starring Gary Cooper and Dorothy McGuire

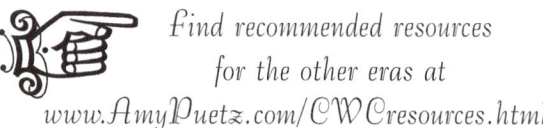

find recommended resources for the other eras at www.AmyPuetz.com/CWCresources.html

Questions about the Quakers

Answers are below.

1. Who started the settlement of Quakers in Pennsylvania?
2. In what year was it started?
3. Can you name a famous first lady who was raised as a staunch Quaker?
4. Name the Quaker lady who made the first American flag.
5. What was another name used for the Quakers?
6. In what city were the Quakers very prominent?
7. The Quakers were very influential in the 1800's fighting against_____.
(A) Taxes (B) Religious fanatics
(C) Slavery

1. William Penn 2. 1681 3. Dolley Madison 4. Betsy Ross 5. Society of Friends 6. Philadelphia the "city of brotherly love" 7. (C) Slavery

Quaker 13

Right is right, even if everyone is against it; and wrong is wrong, even if everyone is for it
-William Penn

Friendship is the union of spirits, a marriage of hearts, and the bond thereof virtue.
-William Penn *Fruits of Solitude*

The Quaker Dress

Collar
- White fabric
- Hook and eye
- Iron-on interfacing for midweight fabric
- Paper-backed fusible web (optional)

Instructions
1. Use the collar pattern below as a guide to cut out the fabric.
2. Iron interfacing on the wrong side of one of the collar pieces.
3. Sew right sides together, using ¼" seam and leaving 2½" opening to turn through (FIG. 1). Notch around neck and clip corners.
4. Turn the collar right side out and press.
5. Iron a small piece of the fusible web on the opening in the back, let cool, then tear the paper off and iron again. This will close up the opening in the back or you may hand stitch the opening closed.
6. Hand stitch hook and eye (FIG. 2).

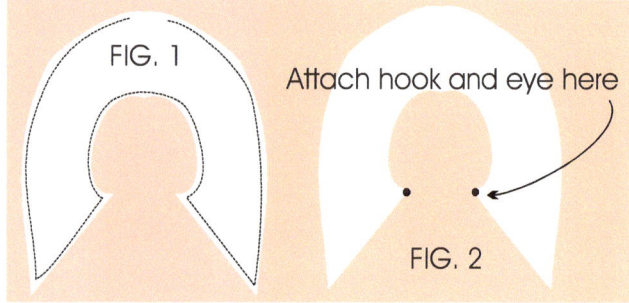

7. To wear, place collar over dress. It may be safety pinned to the dress.

Cuffs & Apron - Refer to the Colonial chapter (pages 7-10).

Quaker Bonnet
- White fabric
- Two - 23"x¼" white ribbons

Instructions
1. Use the bonnet patterns at right as a guide to cut out the fabric.
2. Fold and press down ½" on wrong side of each bonnet crown piece along lengthwise edge (FIG. 3).

3. Place right sides of bonnet crown pieces together. Pin the ribbons for the ties 3" from the top on the short ends. Sew three sides together leaving the pressed end open. Use ¼" seam allowance (FIG. 4). Notch corners, turn right side out and press.

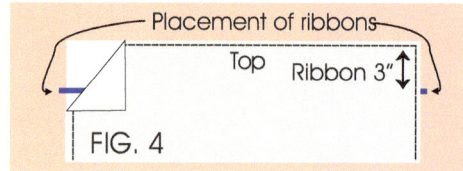

4. Hem the straight edge of the bonnet back with a ½" hem. Gather around the curved edge (FIG. 5) until it is the same size as the bonnet crown.

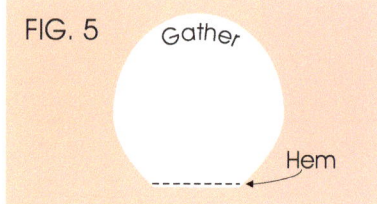

5. Place the gathered bonnet back in between the folded edge of the bonnet hat brim pieces and top stitch.
6. To wear, fold the bonnet crown in half lengthwise at the ribbons. Place on head and tie under chin with ribbons (see picture on page 13).

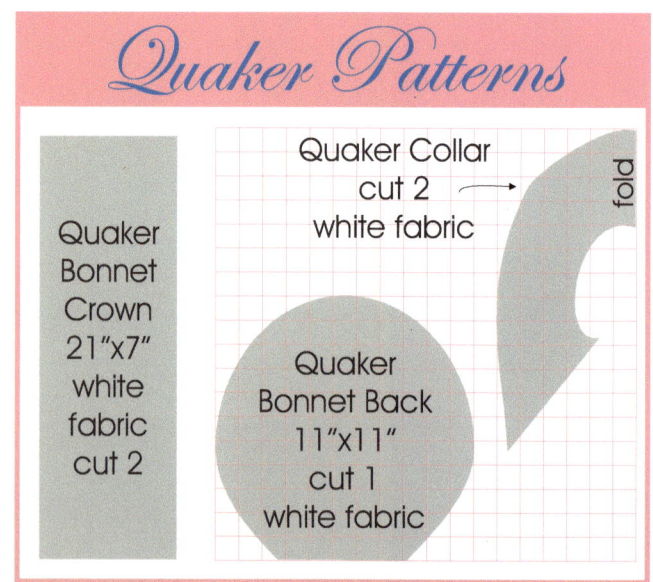

American Revolution
1775-1783

Disagreements between England and the colonist began after the French and Indian War (1754-63). The British government thought the Colonies should be taxed to pay for the war, but the colonist resented being taxed without representation. Many other events and actions led up to the outbreak of war that started at Lexington and Concord in 1775.

Fashions were brought from England and France before the war, but as colonists claimed their independence they also began adopting their own form of dress. Before the days of color fashion plates in magazines, dolls were used to promote the latest styles. A doll dressed in the modern fashion would be sent from London or Paris to the dress makers in America. Soon all the dresses would resemble the new style. For several years hoop skirts that held the dress out at the sides were popular, at least among the upper class.

Below is an excerpt from *Historic Dress in America* by Elizabeth McClellen.

A lady in full dress for great occasions displayed a rich brocade with open skirt and trained petticoat trimmed with lace, an embroidered stomacher and full ruffles at the elbows. Hood and scarf were of silk. No sumptuary laws restrained the feminine taste for rich attire at this period. When the ladies walked out, they threw the end of the train over the right arm. The foot was dressed in a silk stocking, a sharp-toed slipper, often made of embroidered satin, and with a high heel.

George & Martha Washington

When the ladies first began to lay off their cumbrous hoops, they supplied their place with successive substitutes, such as these: First came bishops, a thing stuffed or padded with horse hair; then succeeded a smaller affair under the name of *Cue de Paris*, also padded with horse hair. How it abates our admiration to contemplate the lovely ladies as bearing a roll of horse hair or a cut of cork under their garments! Next they supplied their place with silk or calamanco [woolen fabric], or russel [a twilled woolen cloth] thickly quilted and inlaid with wool, made into petticoats; then these were supplanted by a substitute of half a dozen petticoats. No wonder such ladies needed fans in a sultry summer, and at a time when parasols were unknown, to keep off the solar rays!

The country people of the eighteenth century were rather picturesque in costume. When dressed for church or a country fair, the young women wore flowered chintzes [cotton fabric

George Washington and Betsy Ross

which is shinny on one side and has a pattern similar to a calico] with muslin kerchiefs and aprons. The short skirts showed clocked stockings [an embroidered ornament in the ankle of a stocking], usually of a bright color. Their shoes were strong but not clumsy in pattern, and the little muslin caps they wore under their hats were extremely pretty and becoming. When at work, the damsels generally wore short skirts of a coarse woolen material tied round the waist over a short loose fitting dress of calico, with kerchiefs about the neck.

Mrs. Caulkins in the *History of Norwich, Connecticut* tells us that: 'with the prospect of war with the Mother Country before them, many of the inhabitants of Boston decided upon a non-importation system, and a non-consumption of articles on which heavy duties were laid. It was the practice then, in the Colonies as well as in England, to dress in black clothes on mourning occasions. It was decided to discontinue such dresses, and the custom of wearing black on these occasions was generally laid aside; the only sign made use of was a piece of black crape about the hat, which was in use before, and a piece of the same stuff around the arm.

Molly Pitcher

'An agreement to this effect was drawn up and very generally signed by the inhabitants of the town, also by some members of the Council and Representatives. This would affect the sale of English goods, and none were to be purchased except at fixed prices. At the same time another agreement was very extensively signed to eat no lamb flesh during the year. This was to increase the sheep in the country, and consequently to encourage the manufacture of woolen goods, which were imported from England in large quantities.

'As the great struggle for liberty gradually overshadowed the land, and the sacrifices necessary to consummate the Revolution began to be appreciated, a decided change took place in regard to dress, amusements, and display. Women discarded all imported ornaments, and arrayed themselves wholly in domestic goods. Fine wool and choice flax were in higher estimation than silk and laces, and the hearts of the patriots as well as the laudations of the poet were given to beauty in homespun garments. Gentlemen also that had been accustomed to appear in society in the daintiest costume, following the example first set by the women, discarded their shining stocks, their cambric ruffles, silk stockings, silver buckles, and other articles of foreign production, and went back to leather shoestrings, checked handkerchiefs, and brown homespun cloth.

'The encouragement of home manufactures and the rejection of all imported luxuries were regarded as tests of patriotism. The music of the spinning wheel was pronounced superior to that of the guitar and harpsichord. Homespun parties were given where nothing of foreign importation appeared in the dresses or upon the table. Even wedding festivities were conducted upon patriotic principles.'

After the Battle of Bunker Hill, the colonists everywhere were too seriously engaged to give much attention to the fashions, only the Tories, who persisted in shutting their ears to the spirit of Revolution now rife in the Colonies, and spreading in ever-widening circles about them, continued to import the fashionable novelties from England.

Speaking of the high prices during the Revolution, Mrs. Sarah Franklin Bache (Benjamin Franklin's daughter), in writing to her father, says: 'I have been obliged to pay fifteen pounds and fifteen shillings (£15 15s.) for a common calamanco petticoat without quilting, that I once could have got for fifteen shillings. I buy nothing but what I really want, and wore out my silk ones before I got this.' (Philadelphia, 1778.) A few months later she says: 'A pair of gloves cost seven dollars. One yard of common gauze twenty-four dollars.'

During the Revolutionary period (1775-1783), and, in fact, for the remaining years of the eighteenth century, patriotic Americans who wished to be very fashionable imported their finery direct from Paris, and French taste prevailed both in furniture and dress.

American Revolution 17

I am still determined to be cheerful and happy in whatever situation I may be; for I have also learned from experience that the greater part of our happiness or misery depends on our dispositions and not on our circumstances. We carry the seeds of the one or the other about with us in our minds, wherever we go.
—Martha Washington in a letter to Mercy Warren

Elegant Dress

Country Girl Dress

A patriot without religion in my estimation is as great a paradox as an honest man without the fear of God.
—Abigail Adams in a letter to Mercy Warren, 1775

Country Girl Dress

Vest

Fabric: black or other dark color
45" shoe lace of similar color to the vest fabric

Instructions
1. Cut out fabric using the vest patterns on page 22 as a guide and four strips of binding. Binding for the neck 30"x1". Binding for the arm holes two 19½"x1". Binding for the hem 33"x1".
2. With right sides together, sew the back piece to the front pieces at the shoulders and sides, using ⅝" seam allowance.
3. Fold and press 1½" along the front toward the back to give a finished look (FIG. 1).

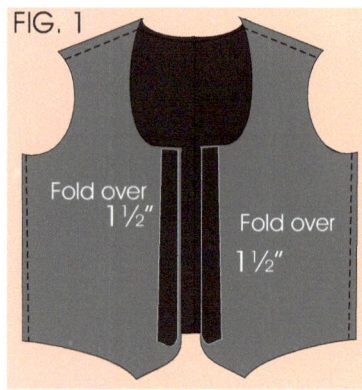

4. Take the 30"x1" neck binding piece and place the right sides together, pinning it around neck (FIG. 2). Sew together, using ¼" seam allowance. Press the binding ¼" in, then another ¼" to wrong side so the binding is not visible on the front side. Fold ends to inside. Top stitch the binding. Do the same thing for the arm holes and the raw bottom edge.

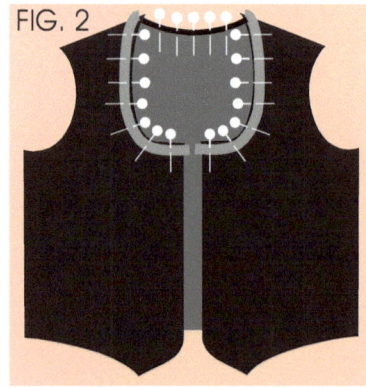

5. Make 5 small button holes on each side for the lacing to go through. The button holes should be 2⅝" apart and ½" from the edge (FIG. 3).

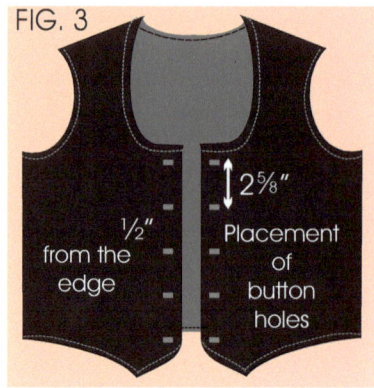

6. To wear, thread a 45" shoe string through the button holes, starting at the top and working down. Tie in a bow at the bottom.

Pagoda Sleeves

White fabric
Two - 20"x½" (or 1") white ribbon

Instructions (make two)
1. Use the patterns on page 22 as a guide to cut out fabric.
2. Take the casing pieces, and press down ½" on the long edges on the wrong side. Fold in half lengthwise and press (FIG. 4).

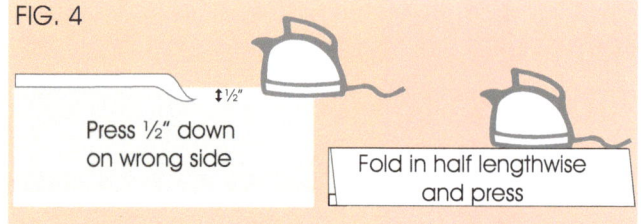

3. Open the casing piece and with right sides together, sew unpressed edges together using ⅝" seam allowance. Leave a small ¾" hole for the ribbon to go through. Reverse stitch on both sides of the opening (FIG. 5). Press seam open.

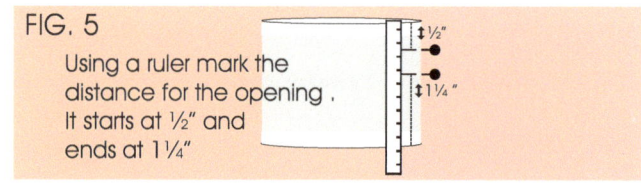

American Revolution

4. Top stitch around all sides of the opening (FIG. 6).

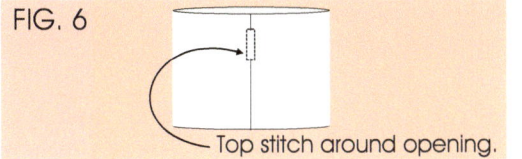

5. Take the two sleeve pieces. Put right sides together and sew the angled edge togther, using ¼" seam allowance (FIG. 7). Open and press seam.

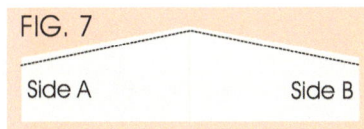

6. Place side A on side B with right sides together, matching seams, then sew together with ¼" seam allowance (FIG. 8). Press seam. Turn right side out and press. All the seams should be on the inside and the sleeve looks the same on both sides.

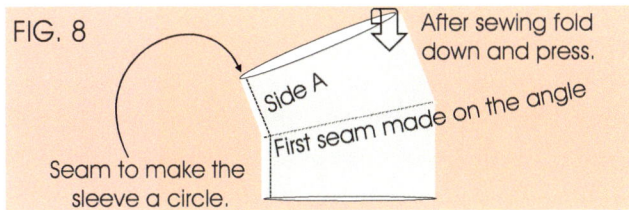

7. Gather the raw edge of the sleeve until it is the same size as the sleeve casing.
8. To assemble the sleeve, place the gathered edge of the sleeve into the open edge of the casing and top stitch. The smallest width of the sleeve should be at the front of the arm, and the hole in the casing should be to the side. Make one sleeve where the hole is to the left for the left arm and one to the right for the right arm (FIG. 9). Thread a ribbon through the casing, or make a ribbon yourself by cutting two 24½"x4" strips of white fabric and sew together, leaving a small hole in the middle to turn through. Turn right side out and press. Thread through sleeve casing.

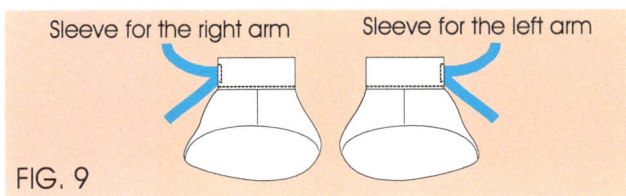

9. To wear, fold the dress sleeve until it is above the elbow, place pagoda sleeves over the folded dress sleeve and have someone tie the ribbon into a bow. The sleeves may be safety pinned to the dress.

Bonnet
> White fabric
> 1" Lace (gathered)

Instructions
1. Use the bonnet patterns on page 22 as a guide to cut out fabric.
2. Take the crown pieces and with right sides together place lace between pieces along the curved edge. Sew togther, using ½" seam allowance. Turn right side out and press.
3. To make the hat crown into a circle, sew the small ends together (FIG. 10), with right sides together.

4. Gather the bonnet back until it is the same size as the bonnet crown.
5. Designate the side of the bonnet crown with the seam as the wrong side. Place the right side of the crown with the right side of the back piece and sew together, using ⅝" seam allowance.
6. To wear, place bonnet on head.

Elegant Dress

Neckerchief
> Lace fabric
> White ribbon

Instructions
1. Use the pattern on page 22 as a guide to cut out lace fabric.
2. Fold the edges on wrong side ¼" then over another ¼" and top stitch all sides.
3. To wear, place over the shoulders and tie in the front with a bit of white ribbon.

Handbag
> Fabric
> 40"x¼" White ribbon
> Fringe

Instructions
1. Use the patterns on page 22 as a guide to cut out fabric.

2. Place the right sides together. Pin the raw edge of the fringe on the inside of the bottom edge. Sew the sides and bottom together with ½" seam, leaving a ½" opening on each of the side seams that is 5" from the top. Reverse stitch on each side of opening to strengthen (FIG. 11). Press side seams open and top stitch each side of opening. Notch corners and turn right side out.

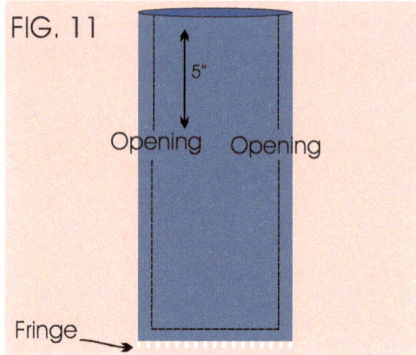

3. To make the casing, turn top under ¼" and press, then turn under 3" across top edge and press. Top stitch one seam on the first folded edge and another ¾" above it to make the casing (FIG. 12).

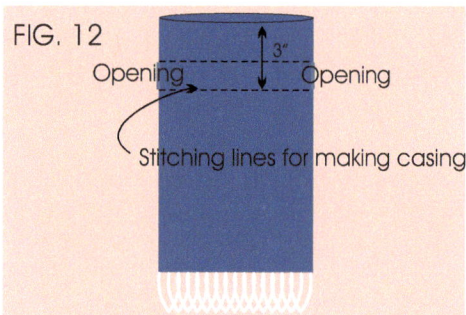

4. Thread the ribbon through one of the openings and pull ribbon all the way around, coming out the same opening. Thread it through again, bringing it out at the same opening. Top stitch the ends of the ribbon together. Draw ribbon around casing so that the seam is inside. Pull out one loop of ribbon from each side to make the handle.

Fan

    Twelve popsicle sticks
    Light weight fabric
    Size 3/32" nut and bolt
    Drill and 3/32" bit
    1" Lace (gathered)
    Tassel (optional)

Instructions
1. Stack the popsicle sticks and secure with a rubber band. Drill a small hole at the bottom of the stack (¼" from bottom) going through all the sticks. The top stick will probably break, just discard it. You will only need eleven sticks. Put the nut through the holes and secure with bolt.
2. Use the fan pattern on page 22 as a guide to cut out fabric. Zig zag stitch around the hole that is in the middle (FIG. 13). With right sides together, pin lace along the inside of the curved edge. Stitch the curved edge with ¼" seam allowance (FIG. 14). Notch corners. Turn right side out through hole and press.

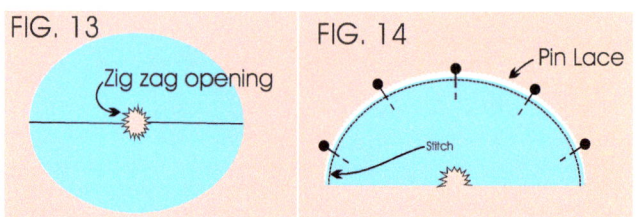

3. Put popsicle sticks through hole and spread them out evenly. Hold the fan up to the light to make sure the popsicle sticks are spaced evenly. FIG. 15 shows the placement of the popsicle sticks on the inside. They will not be seen on the outside as FIG. 15 shows. Pin fabric on each side of the popsicle sticks. Top stitch on each side of each popsicle stick about 1" from edge. (FIG. 16).

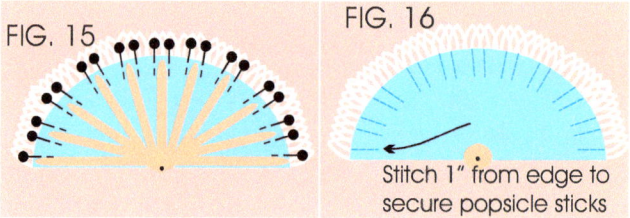

4. Add tassel by securing it in between the nut and bolt.
Another Idea: Larger craft sticks may be used for a bigger fan.

Handkerchief
    White fabric

Instructions
1. Cut out a 12" square from the white fabric.
2. Fold the edges down on the wrong side ¼" and press. Then fold the edges over another ¼" and top stitch.

Underskirt

Refer to the pattern on page 26. To wear, place under the dress.

Dress
To see the underskirt gather the dress together in the front and back and keep in place with a couple of safety pins.

Hip pads
Fabric
Quilt batting

Instructions
1. Use the hip pad patterns on page 22 as a guide to cut out fabric.
2. With right side together sew the pocket together using ½" seam allowance. Leave the top open for turning. Turn right side out and press.
3. Fill the pocket with quilt batting.
4. Sew a waistband across the top straight edge. Make sure ties are long enough to tie around the waist.
5. To wear, tie around waist and place one on each hip under the dress and underskirt.

Another Idea
Use the apron from the pioneer chapter (page 37) for the overskirt instead of wearing an underskirt. Safety pin the middle of the apron and place over the dress. The apron will be backwards from how you would normally wear it.

Find recommended resources for the American Revolution at www.AmyPuetz.com/CWCresources.html

Questions about the Revolution

Answers are below.
1. Who was the lady who took her husband's place at the Battle of Monmouth when he fell?
2. The people of Boston held a demonstration to protest a tax on a common beverage. What was the demonstration called?
3. Which one of these names was NOT used for the British? (A) Red coats (B) Wigs (C) Lobster backs (D) Tories
4. Name the wives of these men, George Washington, John Adams, & Thomas Jefferson?
5. Who was called "The Father of his Country"?
6. Where was the surrender of Lord Cornwallis that ended the war?
7. What document was signed on July 4, 1776?
8. Who was called "The Father of the Revolution"?

1. Molly Hays "Pitcher" 2. Boston Tea Party 3. (B) Wigs 4. Martha Washington, Abigail Adams, Martha Jefferson 5. George Washington 6. Yorktown 7. Declaration of Independence 8. Samuel Adams

Heroes, who render up their lives
on the country's fiery altar stone,
They do not offer themselves alone;
What shall become of the soldier's wives?
They stay behind in their humble cots,
Weeding the humble garden spots,
Some to speed the needle and thread,
For the soldier's children must be fed;
All to sigh through the toilsome day,
And at night teach lisping lips to pray,
For the father marching far away.
-E. C. Stedman

Costumes with Character

American Revolution Patterns

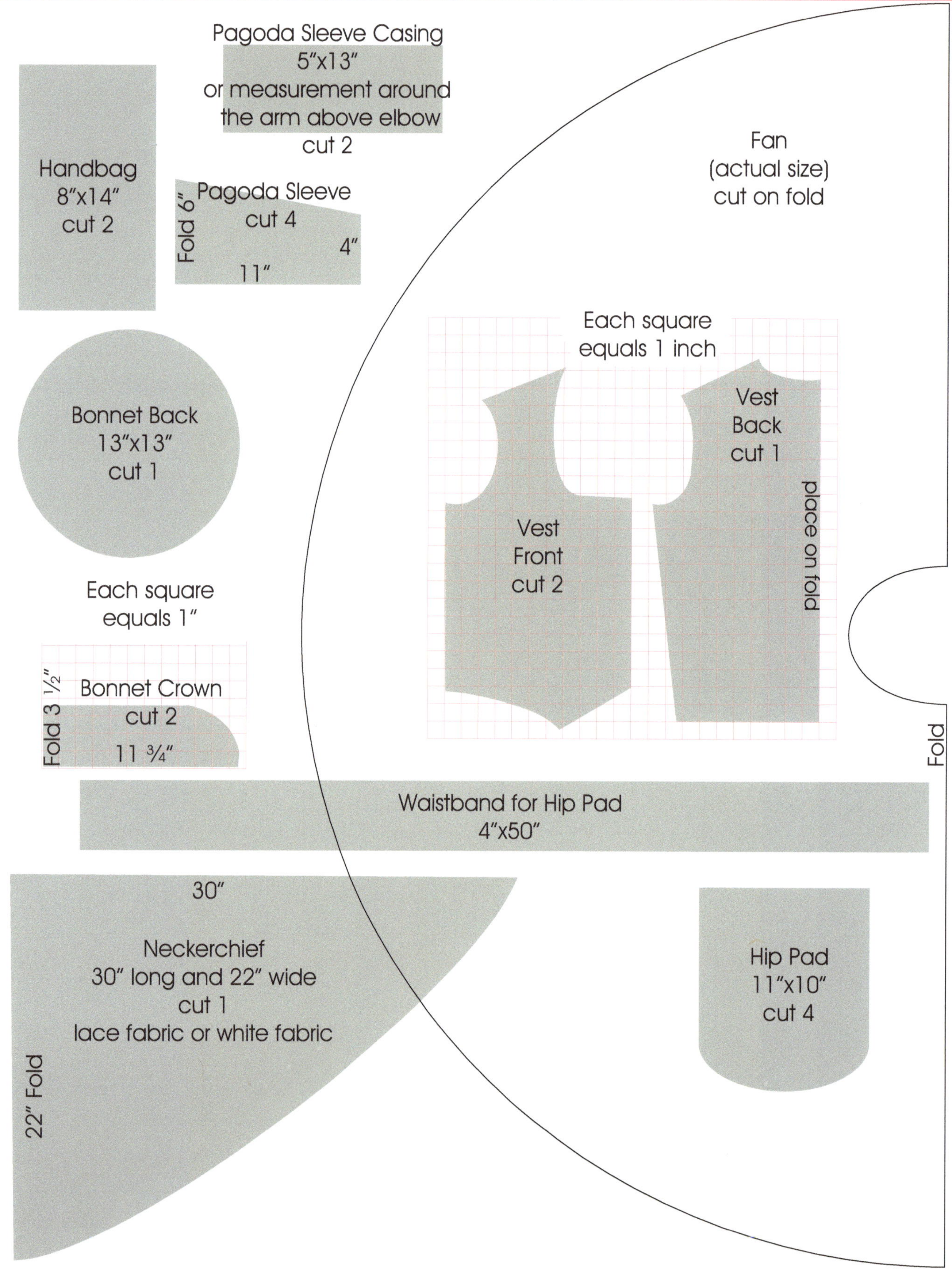

Handbag 8"x14" cut 2

Pagoda Sleeve Casing 5"x13" or measurement around the arm above elbow cut 2

Pagoda Sleeve cut 4 — Fold 6", 4", 11"

Fan (actual size) cut on fold

Bonnet Back 13"x13" cut 1

Each square equals 1 inch

Vest Back cut 1 — place on fold

Vest Front cut 2

Each square equals 1"

Bonnet Crown cut 2 — Fold 3 ½", 11 ¾"

Waistband for Hip Pad 4"x50"

Neckerchief 30" long and 22" wide cut 1 lace fabric or white fabric — 30", 22" Fold

Hip Pad 11"x10" cut 4

Fold

Young Republic
1800-1820

During the early years of the 1800s the United States of America was a young country who tried to earn the respect of other nations. The first war after the Revolution was fought against the Barbary Pirates in the Mediterranean from 1801-1805. The victory in that little-known war brought honor to the new country.

Tension between the U.S. and England continued to be strained. English ships would stop American vessels and kidnap sailors claiming they were runaway British seaman. Eventually the strain led to another war. It was called the War of 1812, but it lasted from 1812-1815.

After the break with England the United States no longer looked to that country to blaze the trails of new of fashions. France became the leader of new styles and they brought the empire waist and simple dresses of the era into vogue. The waistline had been slowly moving up since the 1790s and by the 1820s it began to move down again. In England, the period known as the Regency Era lasted from 1810-1819. During this time Jane Austen wrote her classic tales of country life.

One of the most famous women of this time was Dolley Madison, the wife of President James Madison. Mrs. Madison led the way in fashion for decades. She often served as hostess for the widower Thomas Jefferson when he was president (1800-1809) and became the most beloved First Lady when her husband was elected as president in 1809. Her charm and gracious manners won her the praise of friends and foes alike. On special occasions she nearly always wore a turban. She loved turbans! During the War of 1812 the English burned Washington and Mrs. Madison fled from the White House with an important painting of George Washington.

Below is an excerpt from *Historic Dress in America.*

Spencer jacket with muff

Skirts were very narrow and the ultra-fashionable wore them of very soft, sheer, clinging materials. In winter, to be sure, warm cloaks which completely covered the gowns were worn out-of-doors, but slippers or half-shoes with the thinnest of soles were worn even for walking and must have prevented the 'wrapping cloaks' and big muffs from keeping the wearer's body at a comfortable degree of warmth. Bodices were exceedingly short in the early years of the nineteenth century. The waist line was entirely obscured.

The long and close-fitting stays, though not as stiff and unyielding as their predecessors of the eighteenth century, prevented the untidy negligee appearance the high-waisted gowns would have had without them. As the bodices grew longer, the stays grew shorter until 1819 or 20 when the first French corset in two pieces and laced up the back came into fashion.

In many old portraits we may notice wigs of short, close curls which were in the height of fashion in the year 1800, and in a letter of that date, written in Boston by Elizabeth Southgate to her mother, we find that five dollars would buy one of these coveted articles. They were still in fashion in 1802, for Martha Jefferson Randolph wrote the following letter to her father just before his inauguration as third President of the United States: 'Oct. 29, 1802. Dear Papa, Will you be so good as to send orders to the milliner—Madame Peck, I believe her name is, through Mrs. Madison, who very obligingly offered to execute any little commission for us in Philadelphia, for two wigs of the color of the hair enclosed, and of the most fashionable shapes, that they may be in Washington when we arrive? They are universally worn, and will relieve us as to the necessity of dressing our own hair, a business in which neither of us are adept. I believe Madame Peck is in the habit of doing these things, and they can be procured in a short time from Philadelphia, where she corresponds, much handsomer than elsewhere. Adieu, dearest Father.'

Mrs. Ravenel in her delightful book, *Charleston, the Place and the People*, gives us the following description of the ball dresses worn in that picturesque city of the South during the first quarter of the nineteenth century.

'No more the rich brocades and damasks, the plumes and powder; instead the scantiest and shortest of gowns, bodices at most eight inches long and skirts of two or three breadths, according to width of stuff and size of wearer, coming barely to the ankles. The stuff was the softest of satin, India silk, or muslin that could be found. The hair, descended from the high estate given it by the last and fairest of French queens, hung in loose waves upon the neck until the awful fashion of wigs came in. When that strange mania prevailed, it was hardly thought decent to wear one's own hair. No matter how long, how thick, how beautiful, the ruthless scissors must clip it close and a horrible construction by a hairdresser take its place. The wig fashion did not last long, only a year or two, then came the Grecian bands and plaits with short curls on the forehead, and next turbans.'

Turbans, capotes, and head-dresses of every possible material were in the height of fashion in the early years of the century.

Bonnets were small and close-fitting and evidently of a variety of materials. We read in the *Ladies' Monthly Museum* in 1802 of 'a bonnet of black velvet trimmed with a deep black lace round the front. A close bonnet of purple, or other colored silk, trimmed with ribbon of the same color and ornamented with a flower in front. A bonnet of black velvet, turned up in front, and lined and trimmed with scarlet, a scarlet feather in front. A domestic or undress cap of fine muslin. A bonnet of pink silk, trimmed with black ribbon and a black feather; black lace round the front. A dress hat of white satin, turned up in front, and trimmed with purple velvet. A hat of brown velvet, turned up in front, and trimmed with pink; bows before and behind.'

Trains and round skirts were both worn, but all the gowns were very scanty, the latter measuring scarcely more than two yards at the bottom. (See the pictures above and at left.) The waists were made with a little fullness in front and cut very low about the shoulders.

Slippers with astonishingly thin soles and no heels were worn to match or contrast with the dress, and the long gloves were made of lace, linen, or kid. Veils were long and usually of very delicate lace. Muffs were large and made of beaver, chinchilla, and swansdown. Chintz, lace, cambric, tissue, gauze, silk, satin, and brocade were alike fashionable and worn as occasion required.

In the spring of 1806, large shawls of silk or mohair were much worn, and of various shapes; some in the form of a long mantle, with a hood; others square. Loose spencers [a short jacket that stopped at the empire waist] of pale blue or apple-blossom sarsnet [soft fabric of silk], or of cambric muslin were popular.

Gold chains were in great vogue and a number of rings and bracelets in every possible device were worn. A single string of large pearls fastened with a diamond clasp was much admired, but emeralds and garnets were considered especially becoming to the complexion. Watches were still worn in locket fashion, but they were smaller than they had ever been.

Young Republic 25

Our kind friend, Mr. Carroll, has come to hasten my departure, and in a very bad humor with me, because I insist on waiting until the large picture of General Washington is secured, and it requires to be unscrewed from the wall. This process was found too tedious for these perilous moments; I have ordered the frame to be broken, and the canvas taken out. It is done! And the precious portrait placed in the hands of two gentlemen of New York, for safekeeping.

-Dolley Madison in a letter to her sister about how she fled from the British during the War of 1812

Empire Waist Dress

Skirt

Fabric (print)
1" elastic

Instructions
1. Measure the distance from your waist to your feet, add 2½" and this will give you the length of the skirt. For the width anywhere from 60" to 75" should be enough.
2. With right sides together sew the length edges together (FIG. 1).

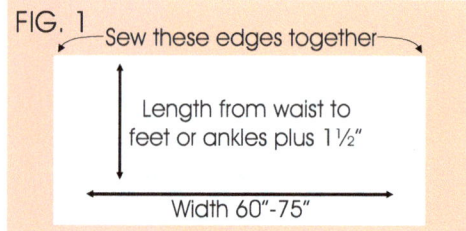

3. Designate one edge as the bottom and hem it by folding and pressing it down ½" and then over another ½". Sew along the folded edge (FIG. 2).

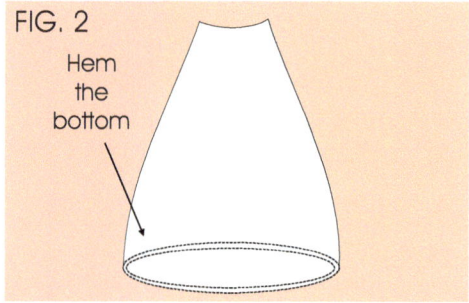

4. To make the casing for the elastic waist, fold and press the raw edge over ¼" and then over another 1¼". Top stitch along the folded edge. Leave a 2" opening. Measure the waist and cut a piece of elastic 1" longer. Using a safety pin fish the elastic through the opening and around the casing. Sew the two ends of elastic together and then sew the opening shut.
5. To wear, pull the skirt over the dress up to the arm pits.

Another Idea: Use the same fabric for the skirt and dress as it will look more authentic. The skirt in the picture was made from an old sheet.

Neckerchief - Refer to the American Revolution chapter (page 19). Make it out of white or creme colored fabric. Place over the dress and skirt to cover the top of the skirt. Place a brooch at the throat to help hold the neckerchief together.

Belt - Refer to the Sailor chapter (page 50). Place the belt over the neckerchief and tie the belt just below the bust. It may be tied in the front as the picture on page 24 shows.

Lace Collar - Refer to the lace collar pattern in the Victorian 1880s chapter (page 55). Place over the neckerchief for a different look.

Bonnet - Refer to the Romantic chapter (page 32).

 *Find recommended resources for the Young Republic Era at www.AmyPuetz.com/CWCresources.html*

Questions about the Young Republic

Answers are below.
1. Who served as the most gracious First Lady during this time?
2. What is the name of the lady in England who wrote *Pride and Prejudice*?
3. Name the war that the United States fought against some pirates in the Mediterranean.
4. Name the second, third, and fourth presidents.
5. The United States again fought a war against England. What was it called?
6. During that war two girls from Scituate, Massachusetts frightened away some British soldiers by playing a fife and drum. What were their names?
7. When the British burned Washington, this woman saved a painting of George Washington. Who was she?

1. Dolley Madison 2. Jane Austen 3. The Barbary War 4. John Adams, Thomas Jefferson, James Madison 5. The War of 1812 6. Rebecca and Abigail Bates 7. Dolley Madison

Romantic Era
1820-1848

The Romantic era was an exciting time in American history as the young nation continued to grow. New states were constantly being added to the Union and by 1848 seventeen states had joined the original thirteen. With each new state that wanted to enter the Union, the question of slavery was discussed. Would the new state be free or slave? The Missouri Compromise of 1820 cooled the issue of slavery for a time.

The industry of the United States began to boom during the Industrial Revolution, which made fabric and other items available to the masses. New technology altered everyday life. In 1825 the Erie Canal was completed. It gave people in the east access to the riches of the west. During this time period, the first railroads were built in America. Andrew Jackson, one of America's most colorful leaders served as president from 1829-1837. After his term the United States had a minor depression, which was called the Panic of 1837.

In the book *Dressmaking* by Jane Fales we learn about the fashion of this era.

Leg of mutton sleeves

The sleeve was greatly increased in size at the top and to it or to the shoulder were attached decorations to match those of the skirt. These gave width to the shoulders, which, with the width and decoration at the bottom of the skirt, made the waist appear, in contrast, even more decreased in size than it really was. The sleeves were usually closefitting from just below the elbow to the wrist. Sometimes deep cuffs were added. Much attention was given to the arrangement of the hair, which was copied somewhat from the Chinese and was drawn to the top of the head and arranged in set loops intermixed with artificial flowers, plumes, etc. Even more interest was shown in the variety and number of the head-coverings. Bonnets and hats were both used. Many of them were military in character, being designed from the caps and hats of the troops. All the hats were very large, with wide brims and high crowns which were overloaded with flowers, ribbons, padded twists of material, and plumes. Many of the ribbons were in stripes and plaids of bright colors. The skirts, although full, were much simpler in design and had little decoration; the bodices were still close-fitting with a very low neck, which was cut widely off at the shoulders. The waistline was normal but more becoming because it had a point at the front. The shoulders of the wearer were made to look longer and more sloping by attaching the sleeve to the waist much below the normal armseye [armhole] line. This fashion continued for some time. A kind of bertha in lawn or lace was frequently worn and increased the effect of a long shoulder. The sleeves were full at the top, but as they were not stiffened in any way they drooped and did not add width to the

shoulder. Many fancy shoulder capes were worn, as well as many styles of long capes and mantles, some of which had hoods.

Except for evening the elaborate coiffure was replaced by a simpler arrangement. The hair was parted and drawn back into a roll which was held in place by a large comb. A few curls were usually worn about the face. There were still many different styles of head-coverings. One of the most popular was a rather close-fitting bonnet with a rounded brim which did not entirely conceal the face or the row of curls at each side. Shoes were low, with an instep decoration such as a rosette or bow, and some had no heels. Boots to the ankle were also worn.

In *Historic Dress in America* Elizabeth McClellan tells about the fashion of this era.

Fashions for October 1830—The body plain behind and full in front, worn occasionally with a pelerine [a small cape with long ends in front] of the same; the frill of which is very deep and full at the shoulders, becoming gradually narrower and plainer as it descends to the belt. The skirt of this dress is made extremely wide, and is set on the body with five plaits only, one in front, one on each side, and two behind: these plaits are of course very large. The bottom of the skirt is finished with a thick cord sewed into the hem. The sleeves are very wide, till they reach the elbow, and fit tightly to the lower part of the arm. Bonnet of straw is trimmed with a band, and strings of broad pink satin ribbon. Large scarlet shawl of embroidered Canton crape.

Corsets proved a necessary undergarment for ladies and Mrs. Hale, in the *Lady's Magazine*, gives advice on the subject: 'Corsets should be made of smooth soft elastic materials. They should be accurately fitted and modified to suit the peculiarities of figure of each wearer. No other stiffening should be used but that of quilting, or padding; the bones, steel, etc., should be left to the deformed and the diseased for whom they were originally intended. Corsets should never be drawn so tight as to impede regular natural breathing, as, under all circumstances, the improvement of figure is insufficient to compensate for the air of awkward restraint caused by such lacing. They should never be worn, either loose or tight, during the hours appropriate to sleep, as by impeding respiration and accumulating the heat of the system improperly, they invariably injure. The corset for young persons should be of the most simple character, and worn in the lightest and easiest manner, allowing their lungs full play, and giving the form its fullest opportunity for expansion.'

A decided change in the style of dressing the hair is noticed in 1832. The low Grecian arrangement in the severe classic taste of the antique is universally adopted by ladies whose profile will admit of this often most becoming style. Coronets of pearls, cameos, or flowers are worn very low on the brow. Gold beads or pearls are woven with the braided hair. The high gallery shell combs are now considered vulgar. In place of carved shell combs, gold combs, on which four or five classic cameos are arranged, are worn in full dress. Another style of hair-dressing which was probably more generally becoming, as it remained in fashion much longer, was a Grecian knot worn high in the back, the front hair parted and arranged in soft curls on the temples.

Black velvet came into fashion for trimmings, for belts, and for wristlets, in 1832, and has been more or less in favor ever since. We read, too, of sleeves made plain to the elbow and very full above. White satin was still a favorite material for evening dresses in 1834. A lady writes from Washington: 'I was gratified by Julia's good looks. She was dressed in plain white satin, and pink and white flowers on her head. Her hair was arranged by a hair-dresser.' Bodices for evening wear were made close fitting to the figure, and generally were trimmed with a bertha of lace or gauze. The sleeves were short and puffed, and gloves were worn reaching to the elbow. As for the hair-dressers' work, styles are shown at left.

Romantic Era 29

America is great because she is good. If America ceases to be good, America will cease to be great.
  -Alexis de Tocqueville

There is nothing so powerful as truth, and often nothing so strange.
  -Daniel Webster

There is no charm equal to tenderness of heart. -Jane Austen

Nor need we power or splendor, wide hall or lordly dome; the good, the true, the tender—these form the wealth of home. -Sarah Hale

Romantic Dress

Bertha Collar
White fabric
Hook and eye
Lace (optional)
Paper-backed fusible web (optional)

Instructions

1. Use the patterns on page 33 as a guide to cut out fabric.
2. Take the 1½"x4" white stand-up collar piece and place the 18½"x4" lace piece on top of it with both of them right sides facing up (FIG. 1). Fold the 18½"x4" collar piece and lace in half lengthwise and press. Give each end a ½" hem (FIG. 1).

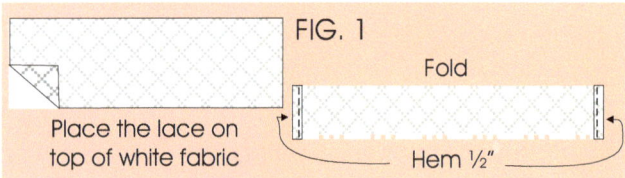

3. Now take the large Bertha collar pieces (the two white pieces and the lace one). To assemble, lay one of the white large pieces right side up, then the lace right side up, then pin the stand-up collar (the wrong side designated as the side with the hem) wrong side up, pulling the neck of the Bertha collar to fit the collar (FIG. 2) and then place the last piece of white fabric wrong side up (FIG. 3).

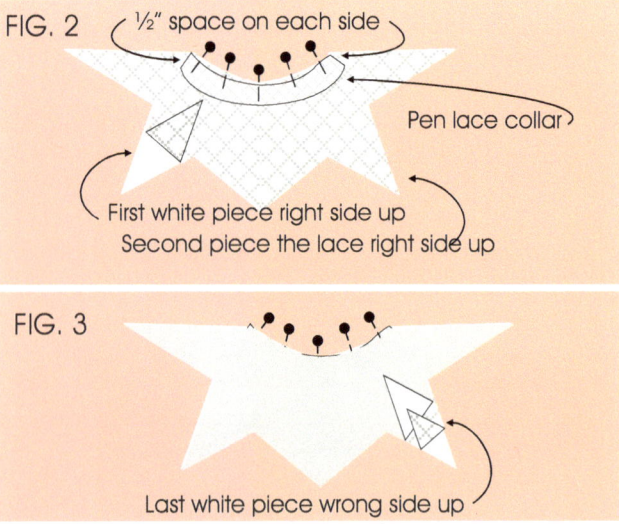

4. Sew together, using ½" seam allowance. Leaving a 3" opening along one of the straight edges for turning. Notch around the neck. Turn right side out and press.
5. Iron a small piece of the fusible web on the opening, let cool, then tear the paper off and iron again. This will close up the opening in the back, or you may hand stitch the opening closed.
6. Hand stitch four hooks and eyes, on at the top of the stand-up collar, one where the seams meet, one in the middle, and one at the bottom.
7. To wear, place collar over dress.

Letter Case
Iron on interfacing for mid weight fabric
Fabric (satin looks very elegant, but any fabric may be used)

Instructions

1. Use the letter case patterns on page 33 as a guide to cut out fabric.
2. Take the 9"x7½" pieces and fold each one in half so they are 4½"x7½". This will help you determine where the center is. Transfer the embroidery design on page 33 to the fabric (FIG. 4). To transfer the embroidery design to the fabric make a copy of the design and place it under the fabric. Use a pencil or a water-eraseable fabric pen to trace the design.

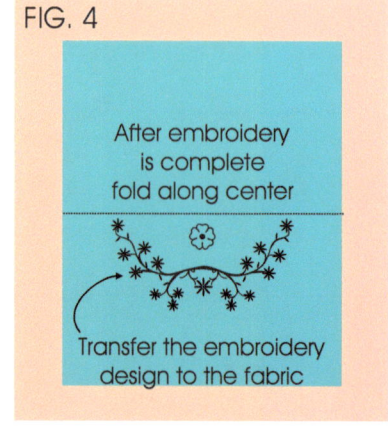

3. Embroider the design on both 4½"x7½" pieces of fabric. Use the Stem or Outline stitch for the vine, Lazy Daisy Stitch for the daisy flowers and the leaves, Satin Stitch for the large flower, and French Knots for the centers of all the flowers (FIG. 5). See the embroidery stitches instructions at right.

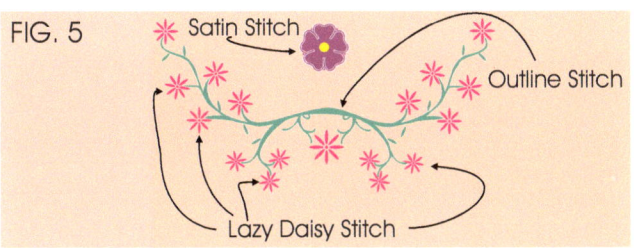

4. Iron interfacing on the wrong side of one of the 9½"x7½" pieces.
5. To assemble, with wrong sides together place the 9½"x7½" pieces together, then place the two pieces that have been embroidered on each end with the folded edge on the inside facing each other (FIG. 6).
6. With right sides together, place the binding on the top and bottom and sew together, using ¼" seam allowance (FIG. 7). Fold binding over ¼" and then over again to encase the raw edges, then top stitch.

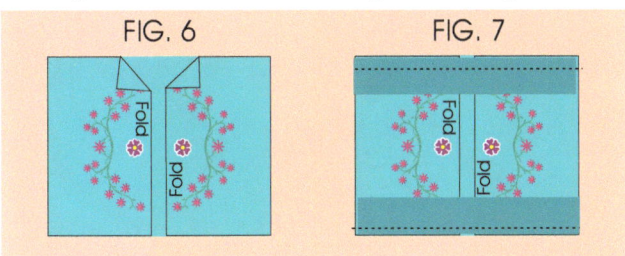

7. With right sides together, place the binding on the sides and sew together, using ¼" seam allowance (FIG. 8) Fold binding over ¼" and then over again to encase the raw edges, then top stitch (FIG. 9).

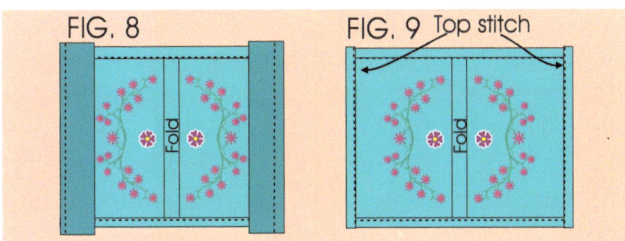

The letter case is a perfect place to store letters, since the measurements are for a standard envelope.
Another Idea: Make a letter case and some personalized stationary to go in it as a gift for a friend.
Historical Note: Letters were the only way of communicating with people long distance at this time, therefore letters were treasured. Ladies and girls would have stored their precious letters in a case similar to this one.

Embroidery Stitches

Outline Stitch: Worked from left to right along the line to be followed. Bring the needle out at the left-hand end of line, let the thread drop below line, take a stitch from right to 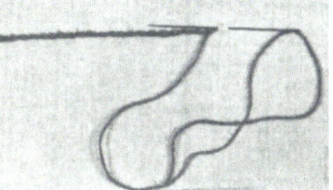 left on the line, one-half the length of stitch to be used, and take up next stitch, one-half length beyond, and bring needle out in same hole with end of preceding stitch, continue in this way, making a long stitch on the right side and a short one on the wrong side, and allowing thread to drop below line each time.

Lazy Daisy Stitch: Bring the needle up at the inner end of petal near the center of the flower, hold the thread under the left thumb, put the needle in exactly beside the hole it just came through and  bring it out at the tip or outer point of the petal over the thread, thus making one chain stitch, then put needle in again at the tip of petal, outside the chain stitch so as to make one stitch over the thread, thus holding the chain stitch in place. Repeat on each petal.

Satin Stitch: Bring needle out on edge of leaf next to worker and put it in on opposite edge, 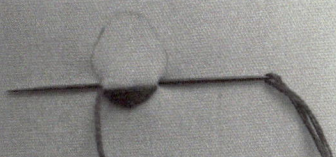 putting needle in and out each time exactly beside the preceding stitch, and exercising care to preserve an unbroken contour of the unit.

French Knot: Bring the needle up to the right side of the cloth at point where the knot is desired, then hold the thread near 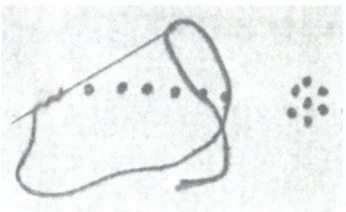 the material with the left hand and wind it one or more times around the point of the needle, stick the point of the needle back into the cloth very near the place where it came out before, push the coil of thread down close to the cloth and hold it with the left thumb, while you pull the needle through to the wrong side. The coil of thread remains on the surface, forming the knot.

Belt - Use a wide belt and place the buckle at back.

Bonnet
    Heavy weight fabric
    Poster board
    Iron-on interfacing

Instructions
1. Use the bonnet patterns on page 33 as a guide to cut out fabric. Also cut out poster board.
2. With right sides together, sew bonnet brim pieces together along outer circle, using ¼" seam allowance (FIG. 10). Turn right side out and press. Turn open, match ends right sides together, and stitch ¼" seam allowance (FIG. 11). Notch and turn right side out to finish bonnet brim. Place poster board in hat brim.

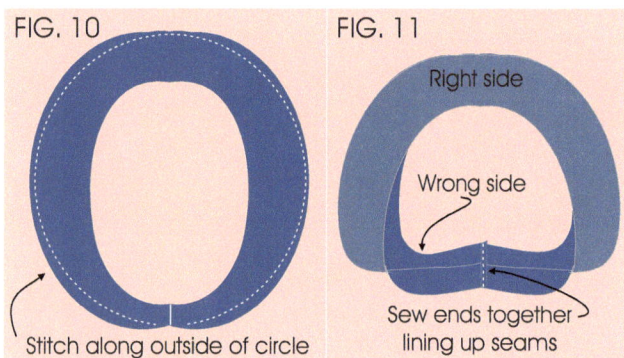

3. Iron interfacing to the wrong side of one of the bonnet crown pieces. Fold ½" down lengthwise along the longer edge of both the crown pieces and press (FIG. 12).

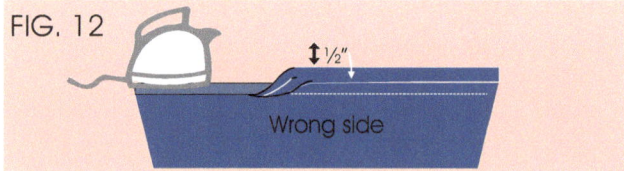

4. Sew the bonnet crown piece together along slanted edge with a ¼" seam allowance (FIG. 13). Repeat with other bonnet crown piece.

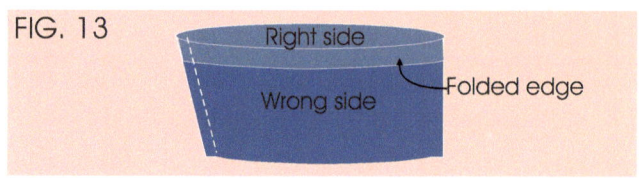

5. Take the ties, with right sides together and sew, using ¼" seam allowance (FIG.14). Clip corners, turn right side out and press.

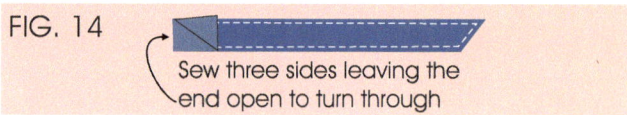

6. To assemble, with the wrong sides of the bonnet crown pieces together, place the raw edge of the bonnet brim pieces in between the folded edge of the bonnet crown pieces. Line up the seams of the bonnet crown pieces and the bonnet brim. Place the ties 3" from the back center seam. Top stitch along folded edge (FIG. 15), then reverse stitch over ties.

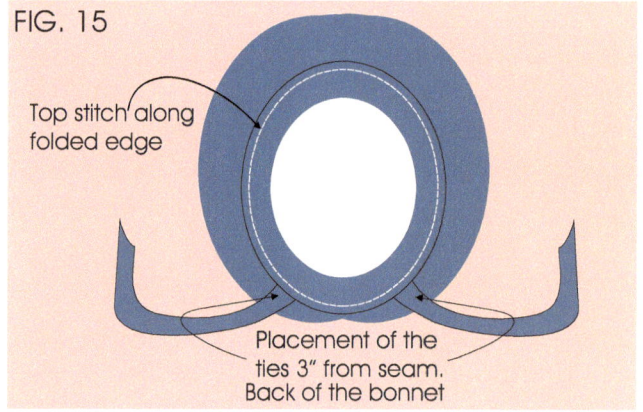

7. Baste stitch the raw edge of the bonnet crown pieces together.
8. Gather the bonnet back until it is the same size as the bonnet crown.
9. With right sides together, sew the bonnet back and the bonnet crown together. Turn right side out. Place the round poster board in the bonnet back to hold in place. The poster board will be removable.
10. Decorate the bonnet with silk flowers, feathers, and ribbons. Attach by tacking to the bonnet with needle and thread. Then the trim may easily be changed.
11. To wear, place on head and tie under the chin or wrap around the chin and tie on top of head.

Find recommended resources for the Romantic Era at www.AmyPuetz.com/CWCresources.html

Romantic Era 33

Questions about the Romantic Era

Answers are below.

1. Name a famous waterway that ran from the Hudson River at Albany to Lake Erie. It helped make it easier to transport goods from east to the west.
2. This hero of the Battle of New Orleans was the President during the early 1830's. What was his name? What was his wife's name?
3. Three great statesmen were prominent during the first half of the 1800's. Can you name them? One was nicknamed "Great Pacificator" or "Great Compromiser." Another was the vice president under Jackson during his first term in office. The last one made the famous speech, "Liberty and Union, now and forever, one and inseparable."
4. What was the name of the Spanish mission at San Antonio, Texas that the Texans defended against General Santa Anna and his Mexican troops? Who were some of the famous men killed there?
5. Where and when was the first railroad built in the United States?

1. The Erie Canal 2. Andrew Jackson; Rachel Donelson Jackson 3. Henry Clay, John C. Calhoun, Daniel Webster 4. The Alamo; Davy Crockett; James Bowie; Lt. Col. William B. Travis 5. South Carolina in 1831

Romantic Era Patterns

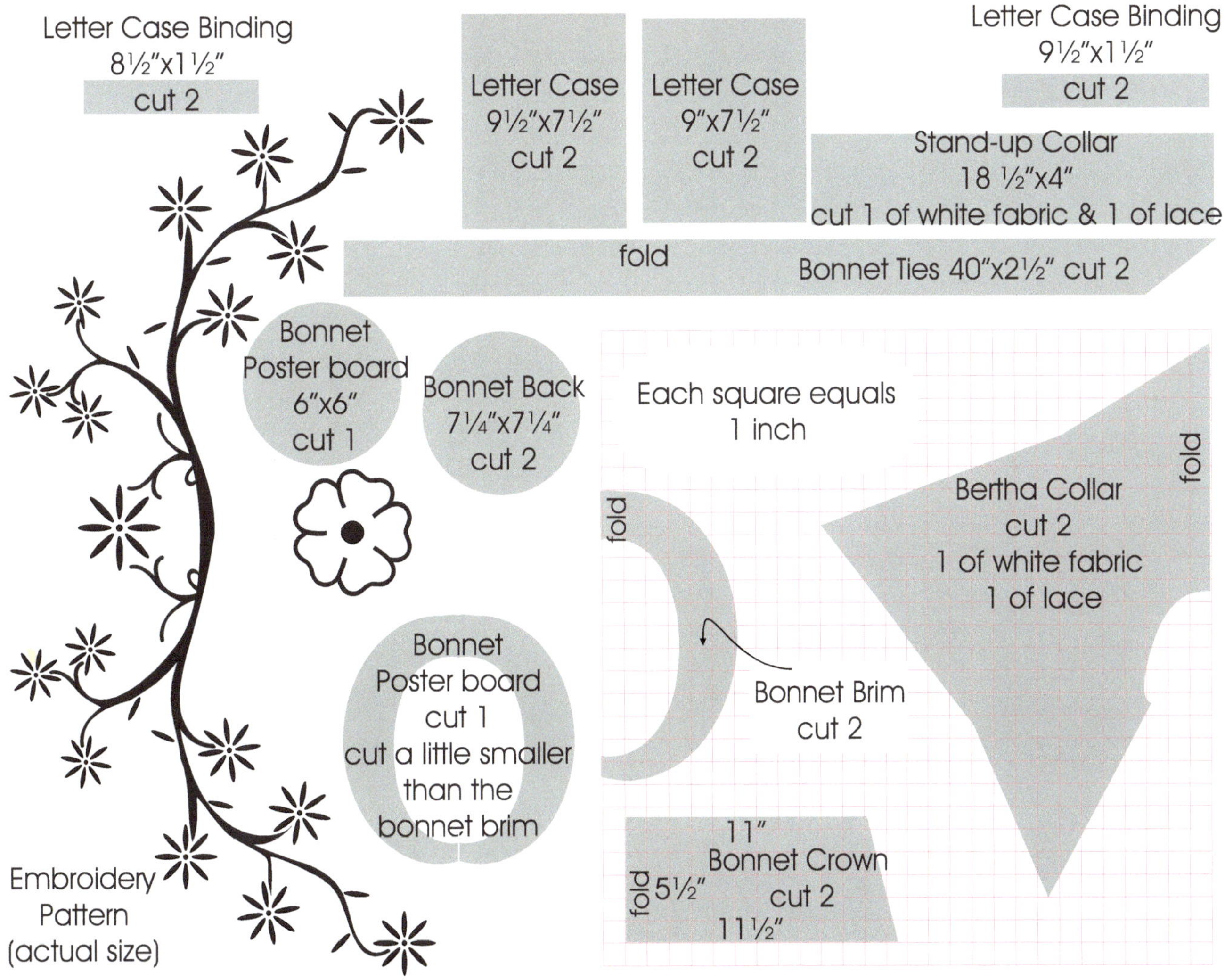

Letter Case Binding 8½"x1½" cut 2

Letter Case 9½"x7½" cut 2

Letter Case 9"x7½" cut 2

Letter Case Binding 9½"x1½" cut 2

Stand-up Collar 18½"x4" cut 1 of white fabric & 1 of lace

fold

Bonnet Ties 40"x2½" cut 2

Bonnet Poster board 6"x6" cut 1

Bonnet Back 7¼"x7¼" cut 2

Each square equals 1 inch

fold

Bertha Collar cut 2 — 1 of white fabric, 1 of lace

fold

Bonnet Brim cut 2

Bonnet Poster board cut 1 — cut a little smaller than the bonnet brim

Bonnet Crown cut 2 — 11", 11½", 5½" (fold)

Embroidery Pattern (actual size)

Pioneer
1800s

The pioneers do not belong to one certain era. From the beginning of settlements in America, people continued to open up new land. These people were called frontiers men and women during the colonial era and pioneers in the 1800s. The most recognizable part of a pioneer woman's outfit is the sunbonnet. Although sunbonnets were popular with country folk all across the United States, the pioneer women are always associated with this simple garment. At Fort Laramie Eliza Donner of the doomed Donner Party remarked.

> Many of the squaws and papooses were gorgeous in white doe skin suits, gaudily trimmed with beads, and bows of bright ribbons. They formed a striking contrast to us, travel-stained wayfarers in linsey dresses and sunbonnets.

William James McKnight says almost the same thing about pioneers in Pennsylvania.

> The everyday bonnet of women then was the *sunbonnet* for summer, and a quilted *hood* for winter. The dress bonnet was made of paper or leghorn [straw made of wheat], and was in shape something like our coal-scuttles [A vessel, ordinarily of metal, used for holding coal and putting it on a fire. A coal-scuttle bonnet is shaped somewhat like a coal-scuttle, usually projecting far before the face. Similar to the Quaker bonnet on page 12.].

In *Pioneer History of Indiana* William Monroe Cockrum tells what it was like for pioneer women.

> Our mother worked from early morning until late at night preparing the needed clothing for the family and doing her household work. The daughters stood nobly by their mother, helping her in every way they could. As the mother grew older they relieved her of the care and weariness of the household duties and went forward in all the needed preparation for the home.

A popular dress among pioneer women was the wrapper, a loose fitting dress without a waist. It could be used for a maternity dress or worn with a belt or apron at other times. William Monroe Cockrum writing in 1907 refers to them in this way.

> The women dressed at all times to suit their work and the weather if they had the material to make their clothing from. The linsey skirt or petticoat as it was termed then, worn over some sort of dress of linen or cotton, made much like ladies wear now for night gowns, was the usual costume. If worn in cold weather a waist or jacket was added to the

Sunbonnets were used for many years this photograph is from the 1920s

Pioneer

Three different examples of sunbonnets

skirt. Their clothing was warm and comfortable. In warm weather they invariably went barefooted, but during the cold weather they had moccasins or shoe pacs, a sort of half moccasin. They made shawls of flannel the same as they made blankets of any color that suited their fancy with bright colored stripes at each end and a heavy fringe sewed on all around it. Later when they began raising cotton in sufficient quantities, they made a very pretty and serviceable cotton dress with stripes of many colors. For head dress they always wore caps night and day with a frill on the front edge often out of the same goods, very old ladies often wore dark colored caps made of some fine goods brought from their early childhood home. They wore the regulation sunbonnet of that period which differed but little from that worn by many at this time. The head piece or crown was made with casings for splits of wood to keep it in shape with a gathered flounce sewed around the lower edge. These hooded bonnets were good shades from the sun and when taken in connection with the other dress of that day were very becoming to the wearer. For handkerchiefs they had small home-made squares of white cotton cloth of their own spinning and weaving. For gloves leather made out of squirrel hides dressed, was used and they were as soft as the best kid and lasted for all time.

When they had wool and linen thread they wove linsey cloth, the best that could be had for comfort and durability. Every woman was her own weaver. The girls who were fourteen years old could spin and weave and make their own clothing. Their clothing was such as they could make by hand. These early pioneers tanned their own leather.

A pioneer family

The fashions of the east made their way west.
The leg of mutton sleeves of the 1830s were also worn in Missouri during this time, as Dr. Walter Williams, the best authority on all lines of Missouri history, says.

The dress of the fashionable pioneer woman was usually made plain, with four widths in the skirt and the two front ones cut gored. The waist was made short and across the shoulders behind was a draw string. Enormous sleeves were worn, tapering from shoulder to wrist, sometimes so padded as to resemble a bolster at the upper part, and known as mutton-leg or sheep-shank sleeves. Heavily starched linings often kept the sleeves in shape, or feathers were used which gave the sleeves the appearance of inflated balloons from the elbow up. Many bows and ribbons were worn, but scarcely any jewelry. Often in summer weather, when going to church and other public assemblage, the women walked barefooted until near their destination, when they put on their shoes or moccasins. Many pioneer women never saw the interior of a dry-goods store.

A pioneer family traveling

Was there ever a journey like this, performed where the sustaining hand of God has been so manifested every moment. -Narcissa Whitman in her journal

I am beginning to learn that it is the sweet, simple things of life which are the real ones after all.
-Laura Ingalls Wilder

I have a freedom in prayer for my beloved parents. Earnestly desired that God would bless them in their declining years, and smooth their passage to the tomb; that in the absence of their earthly comforts, He would fill their souls with His more immediate presence, so that they may never have cause to regret the sacrifice they have made for His Name Sake. -Narcissa Whitman in her journal

Pioneer Dress

Apron

Fabric (print)

Instructions
1. Cut a piece of fabric that is 44" wide and measure the length by measuring the distance from the ankles to the waist. The apron waistband is 60"x4½" and may be pieced if needed.
2. Hem three sides of the apron to give a finished edge, mark center of top and gather top of apron (FIG. 1).

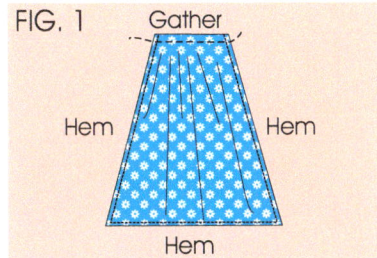

3. Fold waist band edges on all four sides ½" down toward wrong side and press (FIG. 2). Fold in half lengthwise, wrong sides together, and press. Mark center.

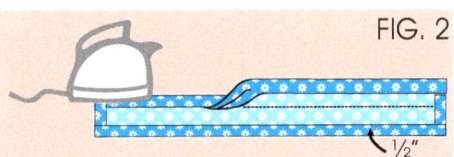

4. Line up the center of both pieces. Place the folded edge of the waistband, right side out, over the gathered edged of the apron. The waistband will cover the gathered edge, pin in place. Top stitch waistband to apron over gathered edge of apron and continue top stitching the remainder of the waistband.

Sunbonnet

Fabric (print)
Two - 10"x ½" ribbon
Interfacing for midweight fabric

Instructions
1. Use the patterns on page 38 as a guide to cut out fabric.
2. Iron interfacing to the wrong side of one of the crown pieces. Press the straight edge down on the wrong side ¼" on both crown pieces. Do this on both the crown pieces.
3. With right sides together, sew the crown pieces together along the curved edge, using a ¼" seam allowance (FIG. 3).

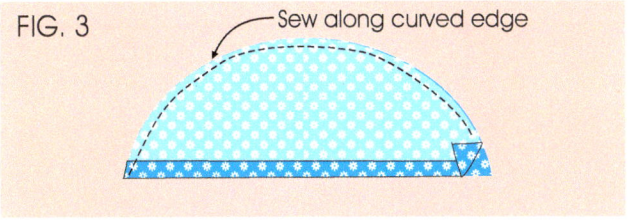

4. Hem the three straight edges at the bottom of the back piece (FIG. 4).

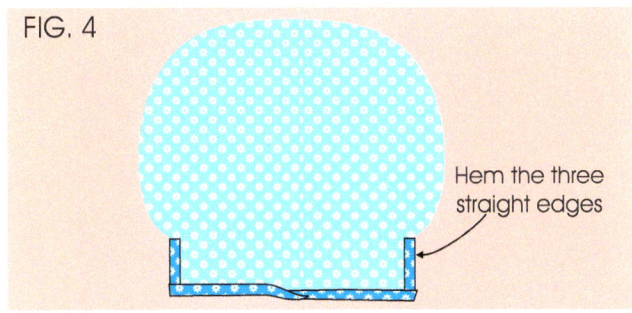

5. Take the casing pieces. Hem one short edge of each piece. Press other three sides to wrong side ¼".
6. Pin the ribbons and casing to the wrong side of the bonnet back 1½" from the bottom. Top stitch, leaving the hemmed edge of the casing open. Reverse stitch over ribbons (FIG. 5).

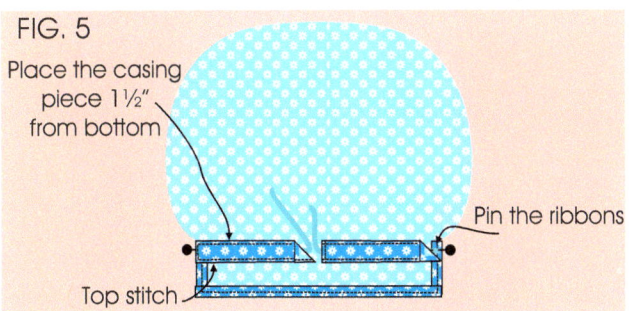

7. Gather the curved edge of the bonnet back.
8. Fold and press the two long sides and one short end of the ties in ¼" to the wrong side. Press in half with wrong sides together and top stitch along folded edge so three sides have a finished edge (FIG. 6). The unfinished edge will be sewn in the bonnet.

9. To assemble place the gathered edge of the bonnet back into the folded edges of the bonnet crown and pin ties at the edge of the bonnet crown. Top stitch the layers together. Make sure to sew through both the crown pieces, the gathered edge of the back and the ties (FIG. 7).

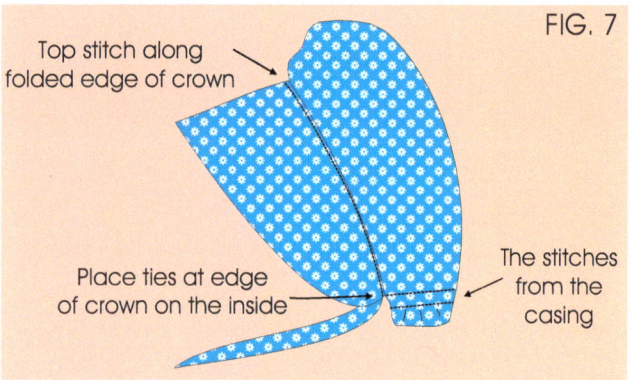

10. Adjust the ribbons in the casing till it fits comfortable on the head. To wear, place on head and tie under chin.

Questions about the Pioneers

Answers are below.
1. Who were the first white women to cross the Rocky Mountains?
2. Name the famous pioneer who wrote *Little House on the Prairie*.
3. Think of two different names used for the wagons that folks traveled west in.
4. Before the Civil War there was a mail service that carried letters quickly from east to west by young riders on horseback. What was it called?
5. This road west started in Independence, Missouri, crossed 2,000 miles of prairie, and ended in the Willamette Valley. What was it called?
6. The pioneers passed through two forts on their way to Oregon. Can you name one of them?

1. Narcissa Whitman and Eliza Spalding 2. Laura Ingalls Wilder 3. Conestoga wagons and prairie schooners 4. Pony Express. It lasted only 18 months. It was a success in the amount of time it took to get mail from east to west but was a financial failure. 5. The Oregon Trail 6. Fort Laramie and Fort Hall

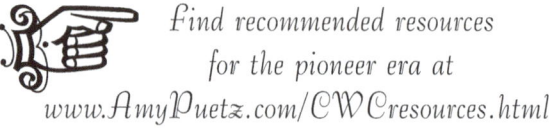

Find recommended resources for the pioneer era at www.AmyPuetz.com/CWCresources.html

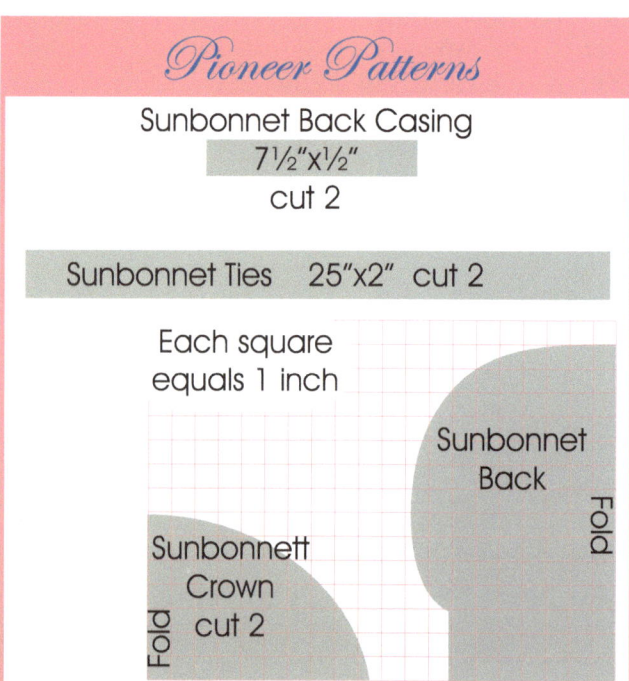

Pioneer Patterns

Sunbonnet Back Casing 7½"x½" cut 2

Sunbonnet Ties 25"x2" cut 2

Each square equals 1 inch

Sunbonnet Back — Fold

Sunbonnett Crown cut 2 — Fold

Civil War

1861-1865

During the mid 1800s the United States suffered through four long years of bloody civil war. Tension between North and South began during the Constitutional Convention but it wasn't until 1861 when true fighting began. Abraham Lincoln served as president of the United States and Jefferson Davis served as the president of the Confederate States.

Women's dress during this time consisted of large hoop skirts called crinolines. These dresses proved very helpful for the war effort. Countless women smuggled goods under their huge skirts. In the North a few sacrifices had to be made because of the war but in the South common items were difficult to find.

Below is an account of the 1860s by Elizabeth McClellan in *Historic Dress in America*.

A hoop skirt

The second empire of the hoop skirt was inaugurated in 1854, and in spite of jeers, jibes, and caricatures held its sway over feminine taste to the exclusion of beauty and convenience. We read that 'the first form of this invention was a whalebone skirt not unlike a beehive; the largest circumference was around the hips whence the rest of the dress fell in perpendicular lines; others preferred hoops arranged like those on a barrel.' But the most popular form of hoop skirt was made of graduated steel wires covered with a woven cotton netting held together by perpendicular straps of broad tape. It was worn in Pennsylvania about 1856. More unassuming followers of fashion lined the edges of their gowns with horsehair and their flounces with stiff muslin. Petticoats were also made with casings around them at intervals, into which canes were run.

The hoop skirt of the 1860s was usually made of graduated rows of steel wire with a woven cotton casing, held together by broad strips of tape running lengthwise. It was collapsible and very easily broken, adding another inconvenience to its use. The earlier form of reeds run into casings made in a petticoat of cotton, proved to be too heavy and clumsy, and was almost entirely abandoned in 1860.

Mrs. Pryor [a Southern lady and author of *Reminiscences of Peace and War*] narrates an adventure during the Civil War, of which the hoop skirt was the heroine, 'One day I was in an ambulance, driving on one of the interminable lanes of the region, the only incident being the watery

Fashions of the 1860s

crossing over the swamps. Behind me came a jolting two-wheeled cart, drawn by a mule and driven by a small black boy, who stood in front with a foot planted firmly upon each of the shafts. Within and completely filling the vehicle, which was nothing more than a box on wheels, sat a dignified-looking woman. The dame of the ambulance at once became fascinated by a small basket of sweet potatoes which the dame of the cart carried on her lap.

'With a view to acquiring these treasures, I essayed a tentative conversation upon the weather, the prospects of a late spring, and finally the scarcity of provisions and consequent sufferings of the soldiers. After a keen glance of scrutiny the market woman exclaimed: "Well, I am doing all I can for them! I know you won't speak of it. Look here!" Lifting the edge of her hooped petticoat, she revealed a roll of army cloth, several pairs of cavalry boots, a roll of crimson flannel, packages of gilt braid and sewing silk, cans of preserved meats, and a bag of coffee! She was on her way to our own camp, right under the General's nose! Of course I should not betray her, I promised. I did more. Before we parted she had drawn forth a little memorandum book and had taken a list of my own necessities. She did not run the blockade herself. She had an agent who would fill my order on his next trip.'

Hats of the 1860s

During the progress of the war, Mrs. Pryor was reduced to finding some means of feeding her household, and out of a trunkful of 'before the war' finery, which had been long stored away, manufactured articles of lingerie, collars, under-sleeves, neckties, etc., which brought good prices in the inflated Confederate currency.

Calico of the commonest kind in those days was sold at twenty-five dollars a yard, 'and we women of the Confederacy cultivated such an indifference to Paris fashions as would have astonished our former competitors in the Federal capital.'

Invention, that clever daughter of Necessity, devised a costume for a Southern belle (for in peace or in war the women of Dixie were always belles) it was a gown of unbleached muslin (made at Macon, Georgia) and trimmed with gourd seed buttons dyed crimson. The becoming fashion of wearing black velvet around the throat was revived in 1860, a gold locket or a jewel pendant usually being worn on it in the evening. Gold chains and rows of gold beads were also very popular.

A prevalent hair style of the 1860s was popularly known as the waterfall. A frame of horsehair was attached to the back of the head by an elastic, and the back hair brushed smoothly over it, the ends caught up underneath. A net was usually worn over this chignon to keep the hair in place. Often the whole structure was made of false hair and fastened on with hairpins.

In the year 1863, the game of croquet was introduced and became very popular on both sides of the ocean. A croquet costume is shown at right from a fashion book of 1868, in which the dress is made with an apron front and looped up over a brightly colored under petticoat and the high walking boots are finished with a silk tassel at the ankle. A jacket is worn with this dress, and a small hat with a long ostrich feather falling over the hair.

The waterfall hair style of the 1860s

Croquet outfit

Civil War   41

I may be compelled to face danger, but never fear it, and while our soldiers can stand and fight, I can stand and feed and nurse them. -Clara Barton

We got to go free or die. And freedom is not bought with dust. -Harriet Tubman

Columbia is but dust and ashes, burned to the ground. Men, women, and children have been left there homeless…and without one particle of food—reduced to picking up corn that was left by Sherman's horses on picket grounds and parching it to stay their hunger. -Mary Boykin Chesnut, *diary entry from South Carolina, 1865*

Blue Dress

Collar
  White fabric
  Hook and eye
  Paper-backed fusible web

Instructions
1. Use the patterns on page 45 as a guide to cut out fabric.
2. Sew with right sides together, using ¼" seam, leaving 2" opening to turn through (FIG. 1). Notch around neck and curved edge.

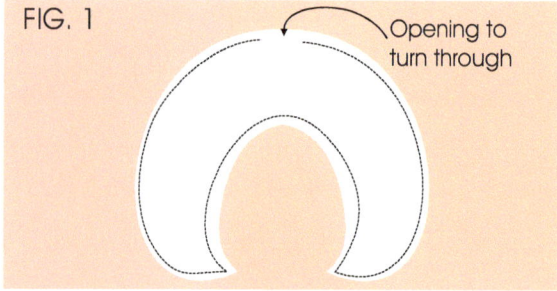

3. Turn the collar right side out and press.
4. Iron a small piece of the fusible web on the opening in the back, let cool, then tear the paper off and iron again. This will close up the opening in the back, or you may hand stitch the opening closed.
5. Hand stitch hook and eye (FIG. 2).

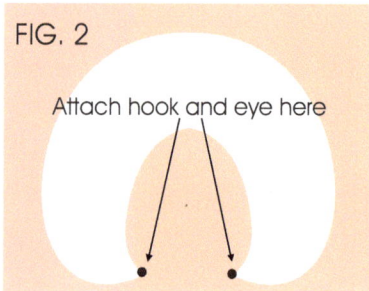

Hoop Skirt
  ½" plastic tubing or boning
  4" wide casing
  skirt pattern (optional)

Instructions
1. Make a skirt that is not quite as full as the skirt on your dress, or you may use a skirt you already have. There is a skirt pattern on page 26.
2. Cut three strips of casing each 4" wide and long enough to go around the inside of the skirt.
3. Fold the long edges of the casing pieces down ¼" on wrong side.
4. Sew one casing along the bottom of the skirt, leaving an opening to put the tubing through. Sew another casing in the middle of the skirt. And the last one towards the top (FIG. 3).

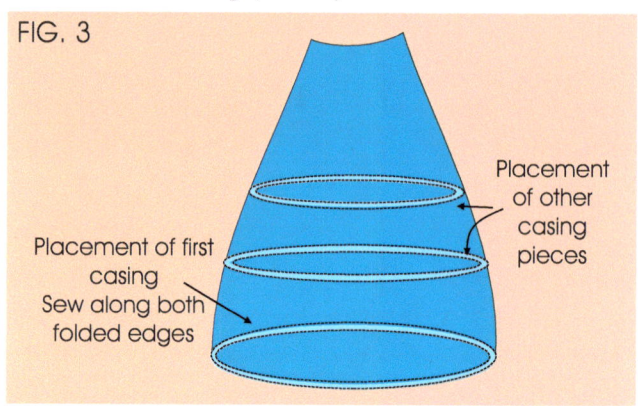

5. Cut three tubing pieces that are the same length as the three casing pieces. Push the tubing through the casing and connect with a splice or tubing connector.
6. Hand stitch the openings closed.
7. To wear, place under the petticoat and dress skirt.

Handkerchief
  Lace fabric

Instructions
1. Cut out a 12" square from lace fabric.
2. Fold the edges down on the wrong side ¼" and press. Then fold the edge over another ¼" and top stitch.
3. To wear, fold by crunching two ends together (FIG. 4). Tie with a ribbon. Safety pin to dress. A brooch may be added (FIG. 5).

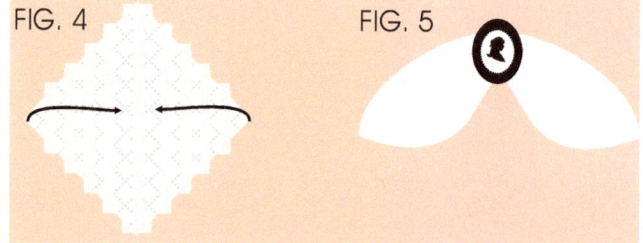

Bonnet - Refer to the Romantic era chapter (page 32).

Handbag - Refer to the Patriot chapter (page 19).

Civil War

Green Dress

Collar

    Fabric (print)
    Lace
    Interfacing for midweight fabric
    Paper-backed fusible web
    Velcro or hook and eye

Instructions
1. Use the patterns on page 45 to cut out fabric and interfacing. Iron interfacing to the wrong side of the collar piece.
2. Cut 1¼" lace 16 inches long. Finish the cut edges of the lace by turning the raw edge under ¼" and then under another ¼" and top stitch.
3. Pin lace to right side, place other piece of fabric right side down and pin together. Sew ½" seam allowance, leaving one side open to turn through (FIG. 6).

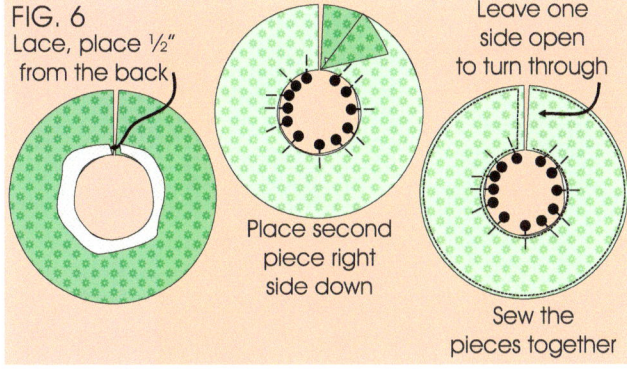

4. Turn right side out.
5. Iron a small piece of the fusible web on the opening in the back, let cool, then tear the paper off and iron again. This will close up the opening in the back, or you may hand stitch the opening closed.
6. Use Velcro with adhesive on one side or hooks and eyes to close the back.

Pockets

    Fabric (print)
    Paper-backed fusible web

Instructions (make two)
1. Use the patterns on page 45 to cut out the fabric.
2. With right sides together sew pocket back together with a ¼" seam allowance, leaving the top open. With right sides together sew pockets together with ¼" seam allowance, leaving 2" on top to turn through (first two illustrations of FIG. 7).
3. Notch rounded area and turn through openings.
4. Press. Iron a small piece of the fusible web on the opening, let cool, then tear the paper off and iron again. This will close up the opening, or you may hand stitch the opening closed.
5. Top stitch the pocket to the pocket back (last illustration in FIG. 7). Follow these instructions to make both pockets.

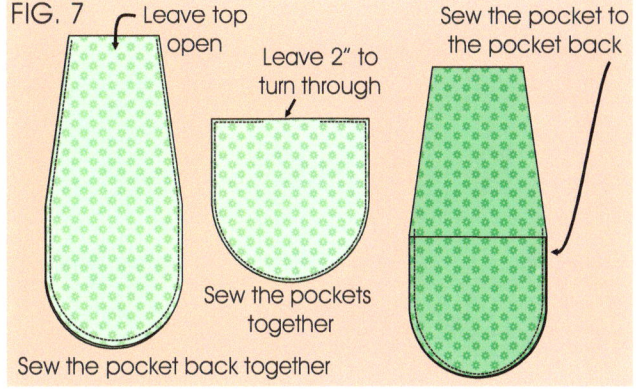

6. To wear, safety pin to dress and place belt over it or top stitch to the belt.

Belt

    Fabric (print)
    Velcro

Instructions
1. Cut fabric 7" wide and at least 25" long. The length can be determined by the amount of fabric you have. If you want it long enough to tie in a bow it should be at least 60" long. You may instead make it slightly larger than the waist dimension and fasten with Velcro.
2. Fold the belt in half lengthwise with right sides together and sew together using ½" seam allowance. Leave a 3" opening in the middle to turn through.
3. Clip the corners, turn right side out, and press.
4. Iron a small piece of the fusible web on the opening, let cool, then tear the paper off and iron again. This will close up the opening, or you may hand stitch the opening closed.

Find recommended resources for the Civil War at www.AmyPuetz.com/CWCresources.html

Cuffs

Fabric (print)

Instructions (make two)
1. Use the pattern on page 45 as a guide to cut out fabric.
2. Iron interfacing to the wrong side of one of the cuff pieces.
3. With right sides together sew each of the cuffs using ¼" seam allowance leaving an opening on the long side for turning (FIG. 8).

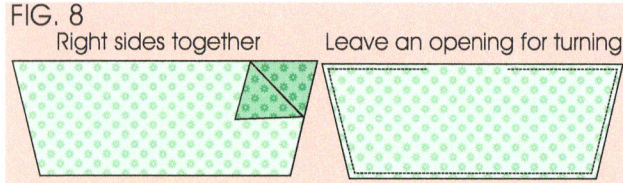

FIG. 8 — Right sides together / Leave an opening for turning

4. Clip edges and turn right side out. Press.
5. Iron a small piece of the fusible web on the opening at the side, let cool, then tear the paper off and iron again. This will close up the opening, or you may hand stitch the opening closed.
6. Use Velcro with adhesive on one side to connect the cuffs.
7. To wear, place over a dress cuff and Velcro shut. The smaller part of the cuff goes on the wrist.

Historical Note: Adding contrasting cuffs to a dress or blouse are one of the easiest ways to give a simple outfit a whole new look. It was also customary for worn out parts of clothing to be replaced. Adding new cuffs to a dress was very practical.

Petticoat

Two full bed sheets
Or 5½ yards 45" wide fabric

Instructions
Make the petticoat large enough to go over the hoop skirt.
1. Take one of the sheets and make a simple skirt. See instructions on page 26.
2. For the ruffles take the other sheet and cut strips about 10-12 inches wide the entire width of the sheet. To make ruffles sew two strips together, then hem one side and gather the other side until it fits around the skirt. Make three ruffles.
3. Sew the ruffle to the skirt (FIG. 9). Place the next ruffle 10 to 12 inches from the top of the first ruffle and the next ruffle the same distance from the second ruffle. It doesn't have to be perfect since it is an undergarment and won't be seen.

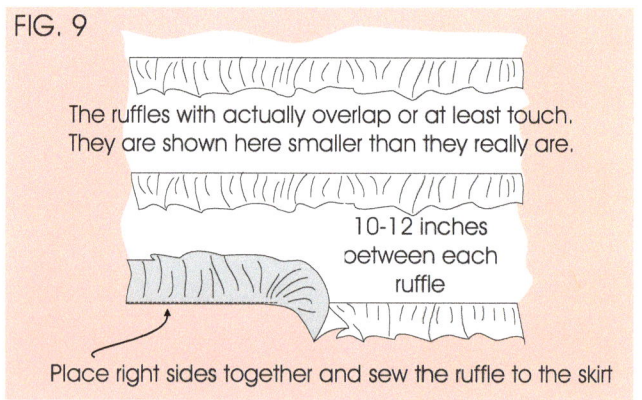

FIG. 9 — The ruffles with actually overlap or at least touch. They are shown here smaller than they really are. 10-12 inches between each ruffle. Place right sides together and sew the ruffle to the skirt

4. To wear, place over hoop skirt and put dress on top.

Note: The petticoat is very important for the Civil War outfit. Without it the hoop looks like a

Questions about the Civil War

Answers are below.
1. Who fought in the Civil War?
2. Name the wife of General Robert E. Lee and the wife of General Ulysses S. Grant.
3. Who was the President of the United States? Who was the President of the Confederate States?
4. Name the book and author that created strong opposition to slavery.
5. Who was called the "Angel of the Battle Field" because of her work nursing wounded soldiers?
6. Name the famous novel that begins with four girls lamenting over their father being away during the Civil War.
7. What were the nicknames used for the Confederate soldiers and the Union soldiers?
8. What were the colors of the uniforms worn by the North and South?
9. Who was called the "Moses of Her People"?

1. United States of America and the Confederate States of America 2. Mary Custis Lee, Julia Dent Grant 3. Abraham Lincoln; Jefferson Davis 4. *Uncle Tom's Cabin* by Harriet Beecher Stowe 5. Clara Barton 6. *Little Women* by Louisa May Alcott 7. Rebels, Yankees 8. North - blue, South - gray 9. Harriet Tubman

Civil War 45

lampshade. Be sure to make the petticoat large enough to go over the hoop.

Parasol

An old umbrella
Fabric
2" Lace

Instructions
1. Remove a panel from the old umbrella by using a seam ripper. Use the panels from the old umbrella as a pattern to cut out new panels.
2. Sew the panels together. Hem the bottom edge and the top hole using a ¼" hem. Sew lace to the bottom around the outer edge. Hand stitch lace to the top hole to cover up the hem (FIG. 10).

Fan - Refer to the Patriot chapter (page 20).

Cape

Fabric
Eighteen - 12" x ½" ribbons

Instructions
1. With arms extended measure the length from wrist to wrist across the front of the body to determine the diameter of the circle. Cut two circles making a hole in the middle and an opening in the front. Make four cuts on the sides about half way up as in FIG. 11.

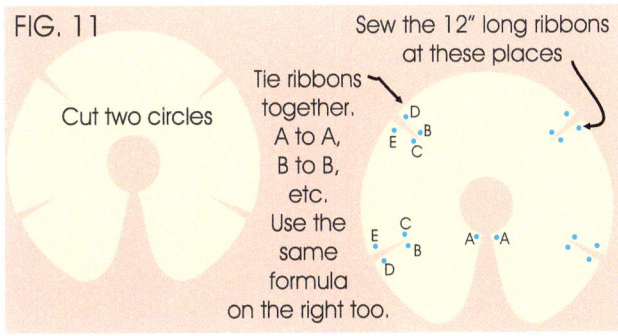

2. With right sides together, sew the two circles together using ½" seam allowance, leaving a 3 to 4 inch opening in the back to turn through. Notch around the curved parts and turn right side out.

3. Iron a small piece of the fusible web on the opening in the back, let cool, then tear the paper off and iron again. This will close up the opening in the back, or you may hand stitch the opening closed.
4. Top stitch 12" ribbons at these points (FIG. 11) and tie together. Once the ribbons are tied together they will make sleeves.
5. To wear, place over the dress and tie in the front.

Another Idea: Make without the side cuts and the ribbons. It would just be a circular cape without the sleeves.

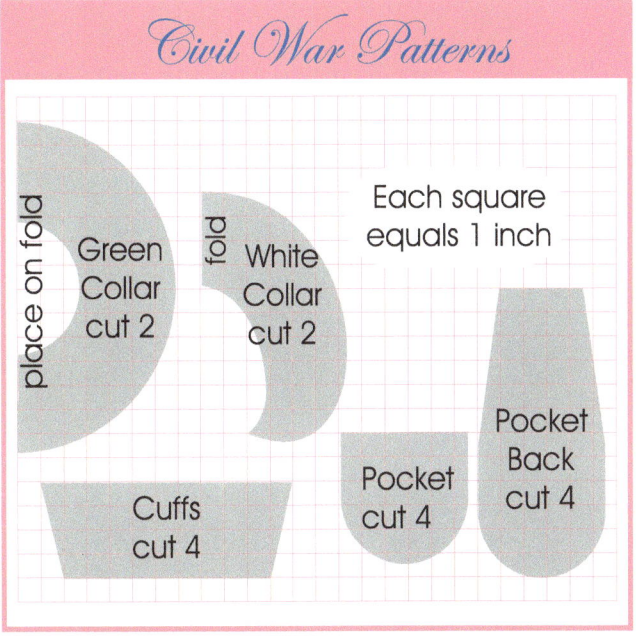

Sailor

1865-1905

During the late 1800s and early 1900s wealthy people, as well as the middle class, began spending considerable time at the sea side. Those who could afford a yacht spent pleasant summer days on the water. It is only natural that the ladies longed to have an outfit that matched their surroundings and dresses with sailor collars became popular.

Below *The Delineator Magazine* from 1902 shares a pattern of a fashionable sailor collar for young ladies.

A blouse with a fancy yoke-facing is a noteworthy feature of the mode shown at right in serge [a twilled fabric], and contrasted with braid. The blouse, topped both back and front by the yoke-facing, is designed to be slipped on over the head, the neck being left open for a short distance. A tape inserted in a casing at the lower edge holds it in to the waist, and a deep sailor-collar embroidered at the corners gives the essential breadth to the shoulders. Plaits confine the fullness of the sleeves, which open with the bands at the inside of the arm. A silk tie is knotted carelessly over the ends of the collar. A sleeveless under-body finished with a standing collar and closed at the back with buttons and buttonholes, supports the skirt, which is shaped with five gores and may have the fullness at the back disposed of in an inverted box-plait (the plaits on the dress at right show what a box-plait looks like) or taken up in gathers. A shield facing displaying an embroidered anchor is supplied. Red flannel with white reliefs and a decoration of white braid would be smart. A very appropriate sailor costume would be of navy-blue cheviot [woolen fabric] trimmed with red braid or finished with machine stitching and an emblem on the shield and in the corners of the collar worked in red silk.

Sailor collar in 1902

The next year, 1903, *The Delineator Magazine* shared another sailor collar for young ladies with their readers.

A variation of the popular sailor modes is pictured at left in an appropriate make-up of blue serge contrasted with white braid and embroidered emblems. The shirt-blouse puffs

Sailor collar for young ladies in 1903

out prettily in front over the belt, and at the back gathers draw in the fullness. An applied yoke in fanciful outline in front and plain at the back is supplied, its use, however, being a matter of choice. The closing is arranged under an applied box-plait at the center of the front. A deep sailor collar frames the removable shield that is finished with a standing collar, and the ties are knotted in a four-in-hand. Tucks turned to simulate a box-plait modify the closely-banded bishop sleeves. A yoke-facing with a row of stitching a slight distance from the edge may be added to the five-gored skirt that is at the back.

Below is a description of a womans sailor collar from *The Delineator Magazine* in 1903.

Sailor collar for women in 1903

A new design for a shirt-waist that is made to be slipped on over the head is illustrated at right in blue serge and white linen, narrow braid, machine-stitching and an embroidered emblem affording an appropriate finish. The blouse, sags slightly over the belt at the back and pouches in front. It is supplied with a deep yoke-facing, and is open at the neck, disclosing a removable chemisette with a band collar. A silk tie is softly knotted at the ends of the sailor collar. The bishop sleeves may have cap facings to match the yoke-facing, and are completed with wristbands. A waist of white flannel might be decorated with light blue or gold braid.

Sailor collar for girls in 1903

There were also girls and women who made a living from the sea. Fashion was not utmost in the minds of these hearty gals but they still managed to preserve the image of those connected with the sea.

The most famous lady who fits into this category is Ida Lewis who helped care for the lighthouse at Lime Rock in Rhode Island after her father became ill. In 1869, Ida saved two men from drowning.

In a biography about Ida Lewis, Martha Louise Rayne, says "She had no shoes upon her feet, no hat upon her head, and no outer garments to protect her from the storm. With only a towel, hastily seized and knotted about her neck, her stocking-clad feet speed her away over sharp rocks to her ever-ready boat."

Her brave act of heroism won her national acclaim. A picture from *Harper's Weekly* shows her with the towel around her neck and her arms crossed in an attitude of determination.

Sailor cap and collar 1890s

Ida Lewis on the cover of Harper's Weekly

Too much sail suits not a small boat.
-Old Proverb

We need to feel the storm that we may know the worth of the anchor.
-Author Unknown

The billows swell, the winds are high, Clouds overcast my wintry sky;
Out of the depths to Thee I call, My fears are great, my strength is small.
O Lord, the pilot's part perform, And guide and guard me thro' the storm;
Defend me from each threat'ning ill, Control the waves, say 'Peace be still.'
-William Cowper

Sailor Outfit

Collar

  Fabric - navy blue and white
  Paper-backed fusible web
  Iron-on interfacing
  1"x24" navy blue ribbon (optional)

Instructions
1. Use the collar pattern on page 51 as a guide to cut out fabric.
2. To make ribbon to go around collar, with right sides together sew a 2"x24" piece of fabric together lengthwise. Leave a 2" opening to turn through. Turn right side out and press. Or you may use a 1" ribbon.
3. Sew ribbon on right side of fabric 1½ inch from the edge of collar (FIG. 1).
4. Cut interfacing ½" smaller than the collar pattern. Iron interfacing to wrong side of one of the collar pieces.
5. With right sides together sew the collar pieces using a ⅝" seam. Leave a 2" opening in the back. Notch fabric around the neck and corners (FIG. 2).

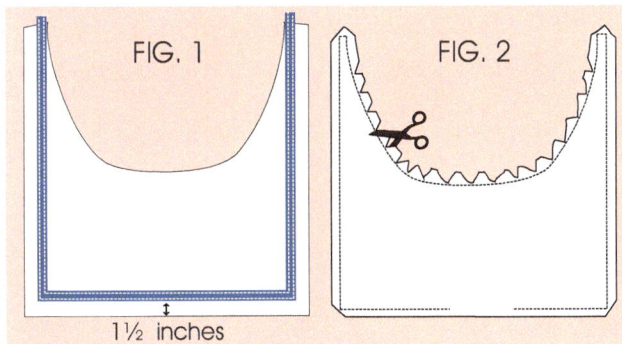

6. Turn right side out and press.
7. Iron a small piece of the fusible web on the opening in the back, let cool and then tear the paper off and iron again. This will close up the opening in the back, or you may hand stitch the opening closed.
8. Tack or safety pin the front together.

Tie

  Navy blue fabric

Instructions
1. Use the tie pattern on page 51 as a guide to cut out fabric.
2. Fold lengthwise, right sides together and crease (FIG. 3).
3. Sew ¼" seam, leaving a small opening in middle for turning. Notch corners (FIG. 4), turn right side out and press.

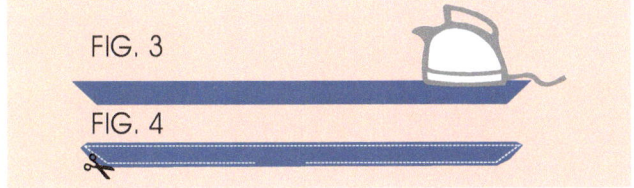

4. Top stitch opening.
5. To wear, tie in a bow and safety pin onto the collar.

Yachting Cap

  Fabric - white and navy blue
  Poster board

Instructions
1. Use the cap patterns on page 51 as a guide to cut out fabric. Also cut out poster board for bill and crown.
2. There are two hat band pieces. Use these instructions for both of the hat band pieces. Press ½" down on the wrong side of hat band lengthwise (FIG. 5). With right sides together, sew each one of them together along short edge with ⅝" seam allowance (FIG. 6), making two circles.

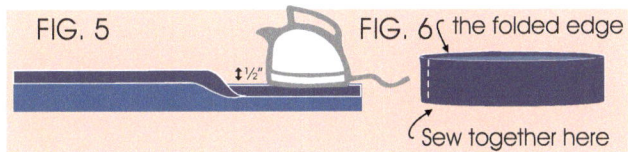

3. Divide the yachting cap crown in quarters and gather the fabric equally until it is the size of the hat band (FIG. 7).

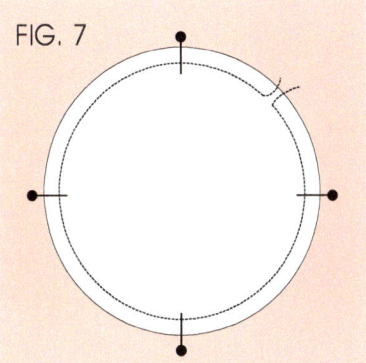

4. Working with the unpressed edge of the hat band pieces, place the right sides of the two hat band pieces together with the gathered edge of the

yachting cap crown in between them. Stitch together, using ¼" seam allowance (FIG. 8). Turn the hat bands right side out and press.

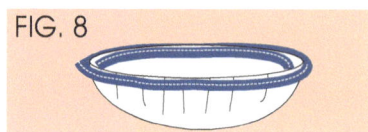

5. Sew hat bill pieces right sides together, using ¼" seam allowance, and leaving the bottom open for turning. Notch around the outside edge (FIG. 9). Turn right side out and press. Place poster board in hat bill.

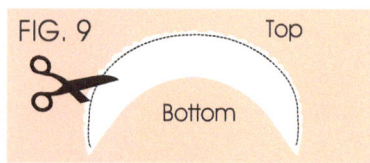

6. To assemble, take hat bill and sandwich in between the folded edge of the hat band and pin, making sure to secure all the layers of fabric. Top stitch around hat band. It is a little tricky where the hat bill is, so go slowly (FIG. 10).

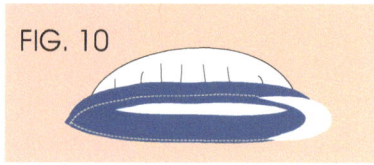

7. Place 1"x36" poster board in white part of cap to hold the form.

Belt

    White fabric
    Paper-backed fusible web

Instructions
1. Use the belt pattern on page 51 as a guide to cut out fabric.
2. Sew together, using ¼" seam allowance, and leaving a 2" opening in the middle to turn through.
3. Turn right side out and press.
4. Iron a small piece of the fusible web in the opening, let cool, then tear the paper off and iron again. This will close up the opening, or you may hand stitch the opening closed.

Questions about the Heroines of the Sea

Answers are below.
1. This young lady saved two men from drowning in 1869.
2. Who was the young lady who saved several people of the SS *Forfarshire* from drowning in 1838? Her act made her famous in England and around the world.
3. This girl was the daughter of a lighthouse keeper at Matinicus Rock in Maine. In 1856 her father went to get supplies and while he was gone a storm came up. She kept the light burning for four weeks. What is her name?
4. In the days before air conditioning wealthy families would leave the hot cities and live for a time at fashionable resorts. Where were these resorts located?

1. Ida Lewis, 2. Grace Darling, 3. Abbie Burgess 4. The seaside

Find recommended resources for the sailor era at www.AmyPuetz.com/CWCresources.html

Sailor 51

Another Idea
Make a large white handkerchief and tie it around the neck to give the look of a sailor collar without actually making one. The one pictured at right is 27 inches square. Use the instructions on page 20 to make a handkerchief.

Sailor Patterns

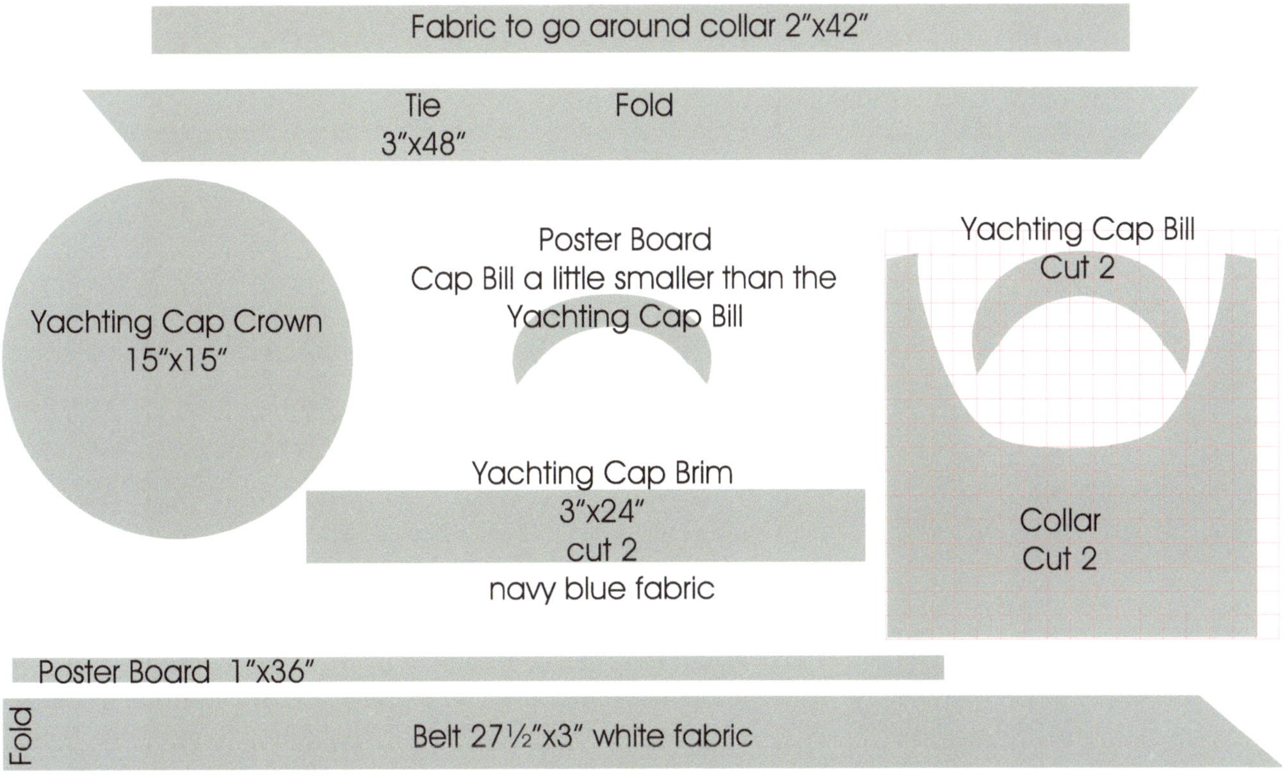

Fabric to go around collar 2"x42"

Tie 3"x48"   Fold

Yachting Cap Crown 15"x15"

Poster Board
Cap Bill a little smaller than the Yachting Cap Bill

Yachting Cap Bill
Cut 2

Yachting Cap Brim
3"x24"
cut 2
navy blue fabric

Collar
Cut 2

Poster Board 1"x36"

Fold   Belt 27½"x3" white fabric

Victorian
1880s

This era in history is sometimes called The Gilded Age because of the prosperity and growth that took place. Social reforms were blooming everywhere. Many women became active in trying to improve the conditions of the poor and needy. A great tragedy hit the country during the beginning of the decade when the 20th President, James A. Garfield, was assassinated. The country recovered from this shock and celebrated other exciting events, including the arrival of the Statue of Liberty in 1886.

In dress the prevailing look of the decade was the bustle. By the mid 1880s bustles reached an extravagant size. Bustles were made of fabric or steel and held out the dress at the back. It was also called a dress improver.

London and Paris still led the way in fashion. At the beginning of the decade the skirts were tight around the legs which made small lady-like steps a necessity. This carried over from the fashions of the 1870s but by the mid to late 1880s the skirts were wider and the bustle continued to grow. The top picture on the next page show how large the bustles were. The picture at right shows the tight shirts with the numerous trimmings and folds of fabric that accompanied them. The dress consisted of an underskirt and overskirt, which were sometimes of different fabric but more often of the same material. Large sashes were in vogue [see the pictures top and middle pictures on the next page]. Lace collars were extremely popular.

1881 Fashions

Parasols, just like the bustle, began small and grew as the decade progressed. Compare the parasol above to the one on the next page.

In the middle of the decade a tailor made suit for women became the fashion. This outfit consisted of a skirt and a tight fitting jacket to match. Women wore a corset and petticoats along with their bustle.

Skating may seem like a modern activity, but the ladies and girls of the 1870s and 1880s enjoyed it too. They even had costumes to wear while skating.

Here is a description for the dress above (on the right) from *The London and Paris Ladies' Magazine of Fashion* from 1881.

Skating outfits

Elegant Promenade Costume of black satin and Pekin [a silk fabric with wide stripes]. The jacket is of purple satin, double-breasted, and trimmed with a deep plisse [a puckered type of pleat]: the skirt is composed of a long plisse in front, and three small

Victorian 1880s   53

plisses on each side, trimmed by a drapery of Pekin, which forms bows and ends on the left side, each end being trimmed by a bow; the right side of this dress is slightly draped.

In the spring of 1885 weekly journal, *Household Words* gave this advice about clothing.

Dolman (left)

For outdoor wear in spring, as soon as sealskin jackets and heavy dolmans [a type of coat with cape like sleeves] may be dispensed with, an intermediate kind of dress will be worn to fill up the interval until summer dresses come in. The shape is that of a princess dress with full puffed out back, while the front opens, showing a vest in the bodice and a simulated petticoat in the skirt. Round the petticoat hem a full pleating or frilling must show the upper skirt, which may be plain, or full. The vests, as at present designed, are of colors contrasting or harmonizing with the dress, and of material slighter and less costly. The fronts of the tunic, which hang loosely and are not sewed down upon the skirt, require silk lining.

Tailored Dress of the 1880s

Here is a description for the picture below from *The London and Paris Ladies' Magazine of Fashion* from 1881.

This afternoon tea gown (left in the picture below) is of dove-colored cashmere, trimmed with blue satin and white lace. The dress is made in princess form, with a decorative piece in front, edged with lace, and has a pointed belt: the collar and sleeves are very pretty.

This dress (the middle one pictured below) is trimmed with red satin ribbon of the shade called Princess of Wales's. The body is gathered front and back, and trimmed with a handsome lace collar: the overskirt is laid in pleats in front, and is elegantly draped behind; it is trimmed all round with a satin ruching, a fringe, and lace. The underskirt consists of lace or embroidered flounces.

An elegant dinner dress of olive-green satin, trimmed with brocade [fabric woven with a raised or enriched design of flowers, foliage, and other ornaments.] is on the right in the picture at right. The low waist of the dress is pointed back and front, edged by two cross folds of satin, which may be of the same color as the sash, or olive-green, as represented on the plate: the underskirt is composed of wide tads of brocade and pleats of satin, crossed by draperies of the same: the back is well puffed and ornamented by a long sash, matching in color the flowers of the brocade.

1881 Fashions

54 ~ Costumes with Character

*If the power to do hard work is not a skill, it's the best possible substitute for it.
If wrinkles must be written upon our brows, let them not be written upon the heart.* -James A. Garfield

No Christian nation can be considered great which ignores the Sacred Book. -Fanny Crosby

The spirit should never grow old. -James A. Garfield

I am most anxious to enlist everyone who can speak or write to join in checking this mad, wicked folly of 'Women's Rights,' with all its attendant horrors, on which her poor feeble sex is bent, forgetting every sense of womanly feeling and propriety. Feminists ought to get a good whipping. -Queen Victoria

Victorian 1880s

Square Collar Dress

Square Ruffle Collar
Iron-on interfacing
1" flat lace
Four hooks and eyes
Fabric same color as the dress

Instructions

1. Use the ruffle collar patterns on page 57 as a guide to cut out fabric. Also cut the 1" lace 51" long.
2. Take the lace and gather so it will fit on the stand-up neck collar. Hem each end of the lace with ¼" hem.
3. Iron the interfacing to the stand-up neck collar piece. With right sides together, sew three sides of the collar pieces together with the lace at the top, using ¼" seam allowance (FIG. 1). Notch corners and turn right side out.

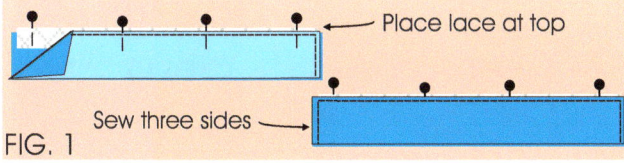

4. Take the ruffle and give three sides a ½" finished hem (FIG. 2). Gather the raw edge.

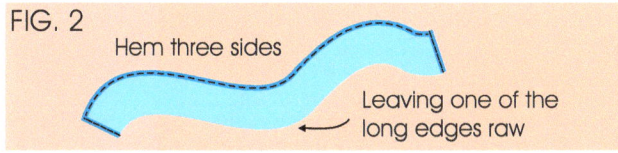

5. Iron interfacing to the wrong side of one the collar pieces. Pin the stand-up collar piece and the ruffle in between the two larger collar pieces (FIG. 3).

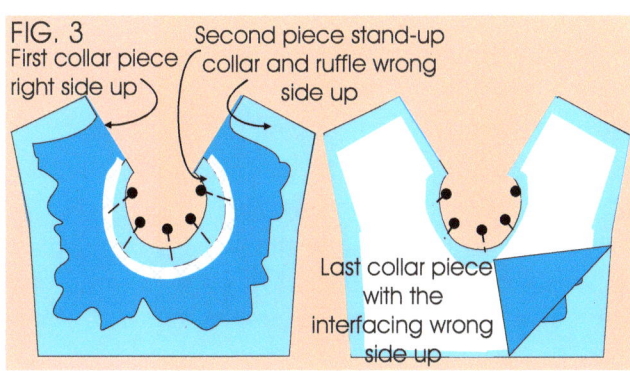

6. Sew the collar with the lace to the neck of the collar, using ¼" seam allowance. You may need to pull the neckline straight. Sew the remainder of the collar, using ¼" seam allowance, and leaving a 3" opening in the front to turn through.

7. Clip corners and notch neck if necessary, then turn right side out. Top stitch opening with thread the same color as the collar.
8. Sew a piece of 1" lace on where the collar and ruffle meet. Attach hooks and eyes (FIG 4).

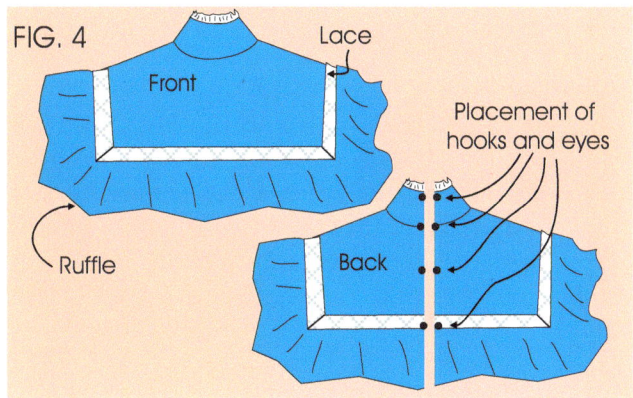

9. To wear, place over dress and connect hooks and eyes.

Lace Collar Dress

Lace Collar
White fabric
5" wide lace 40" long
36"x ½" ribbon

Instructions

1. Cut 5" lace 40" long. Cut out white fabric 6"x40". Cut out casing 2"x40".
2. Take the 6"x40" piece of white fabric and fold the top and bottom edges down ¼", then over another ¼" and press (FIG. 5). Place right side of white fabric on wrong side of lace and fold the two short edges of both the lace and white fabric to wrong side ¼", then over another ¼". Top stitch all four sides of white fabric and lace (FIG. 6).

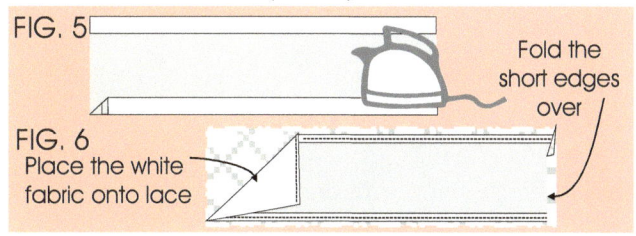

3. Take the 2"x40" piece of casing. Fold and press ¼" to wrong side of top and bottom. Fold the right and left ends over to wrong side ¼", then over another ¼" and topstitch.
4. Place the casing on the collar, wrong sides together, 1" from top. Top stitch the top and the

bottom of the casing to the lace and fabric pieces (FIG. 7). Thread a ribbon into the casing.

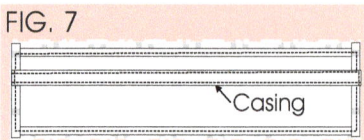

5. To wear, place at throat and tie ribbon into a bow.
Alternate Instructions: If you do not have 5" lace, fabric lace may be used. Just cut the lace the same size as the white fabric piece. Place the wrong side of lace to the right side of white fabric and fold all four edges over ¼", then over another ¼" and top stitch then follow the instructions in step 3 - 5 to finish the collar.

Lace Cuffs
White fabric
5" wide lace
Elastic

Instructions (make two)
1. Cut 5" lace 40" long. Cut out white fabric 6"x40". Cut out casing 2"x40".
2. Fold and press down ¼", then over another ¼" and press on wrong side along top and bottom of the long edge of white fabric. Place right side of white fabric on wrong side of lace. Top stitch the top and the bottom together (FIG. 8).
3. Take the 2"x40" piece of fabric. Fold and press ¼" to wrong side of top and bottom. Fold the short edges over to wrong side ¼", then over another ¼" and top stitch.
4. Place the casing on the cuff, wrong sides together, 1" from top. Top stitch the top and the bottom of the casing (FIG. 8).

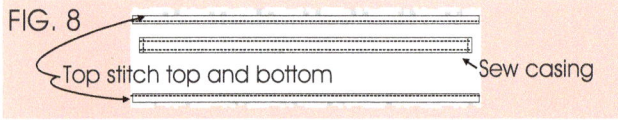

5. With right sides together, sew the ends together using a ½" seam.
6. Thread ½" wide elastic into the casing (the elastic should be the circumference of the wrist plus ½") and stitch elastic together.
7. To wear, place lace cuff over the dress cuff.
Alternate Instructions: If you do not have 5" lace, fabric lace may be used. Cut the lace the same size as the white fabric piece. Place the wrong side of lace on the right side of white fabric and fold the top and the bottom of the long edge over and top stitch, then follow the instructions in step 3 - 7 to finish the cuffs.

Questions about the 1880s

Answers are below.
1. Name the famous monument that France gave to the United States in 1886.
2. Name the famous girl of the Wild, Wild, West Shows, who was called "Little Miss Sure Shot."
3. Who was the 20th President of the United States? He was a minister of the gospel and was assassinated in 1881. He was the second president to be assassinated.
4. What was the name of a blind lady who wrote over eight thousand beloved hymns such as *All the Way My Savior Leads Me* and *To God be the Glory*?
5. In 1882 this inventor of the light bulb lit up the financial district of New York City. What was his name?
6. The 1880s were a time of prosperity spurred on by the industrialization that took place after the Civil War. What was the name that Mark Twain gave this era?

1. The Statue of Liberty 2. Annie Oakley 3. James A. Garfield 4. Fanny Crosby 5. Thomas Alva Edison 6. The Gilded Age. In 1873 he wrote a book by that name and the prosperity continued till the 1890s

Parasol - Refer to the Civil War chapter (page 45).

Belt - Refer to the Sailor chapter (page 50).

Bustle - Refer to the Patriot chapter (page 21) for the hip pads. To wear, place the two pads in the back on top of each other or next to each other and tie around the front. Place underskirt and dress skirt over the bustle.

Underskirt
Use a skirt you already have that is of a coordinating color to the dress as the underskirt. Or make one, see page 26 for instructions. Pull the sides of the dress

skirt up and pin with safety pins (see picture on page 54).

Name Cards
- Paper cutter or scissors
- Colored or textured card stock
- Computer program that makes business cards

Instructions

1. Open computer program and set the page to business cards, using the Avery size 5371. Now add a flower clip art, then under the flowers write your full name in an elegant-looking text. Print the name cards on the card stock. For an example, see picture.

2. To cut the paper. Cut off ¾" on the two long sides and cut off ½" on the top and bottom. Next cut the page down the middle, then cut each card 2" high (FIG 9). Or use perforated business card paper.

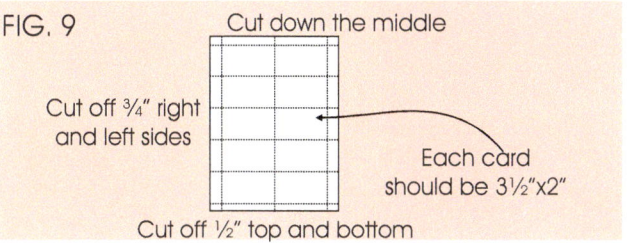

Historical Note: Every Victorian lady owned calling cards. In the afternoon calls would be made or a lady would stay at home to receive calls. A lady would always leave a calling card. Messages could be left by folding a corner of the card. <u>Correct Social Usage</u> published in 1905 offers this advice, "Until about 1895, ladies, when paying calls that proved fruitless, left behind at each house one card with its left end bent toward the center to indicate that all the feminine members of the family were included in the call."

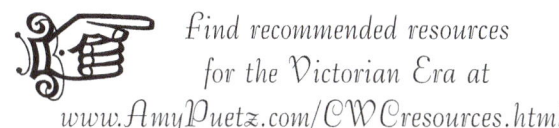

Find recommended resources for the Victorian Era at www.AmyPuetz.com/CWCresources.html

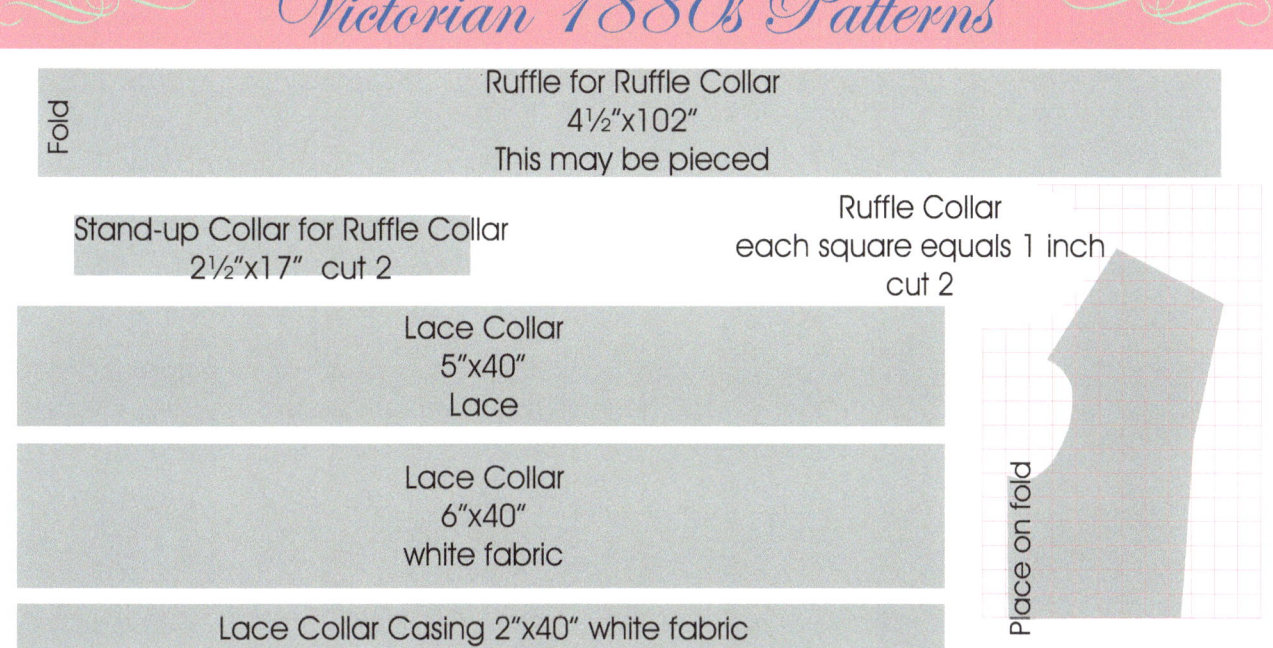

Victorian

1890s

The United States continued to be a growing and prosperous country. There was a minor set back during the panic of 1893 but by the end of the decade the economy was sound. During the last years of the decade the United States fought a war against Spain on the island of Cuba. The Spanish-American War was remembered as a "splendid little war." New inventions were being made by men like Henry Ford, who made his first automobile in 1896, and Thomas Edison, who patented the first moving picture camera in 1891.

This decade's fashions were much simpler than the preceding ones. The bustle disappeared and lighter petticoats were worn under the elegant dresses. Puffed sleeves again showed themselves, they were tight around the lower arm and then ballooned out from the elbow up. They were called leg of mutton sleeves because they resembled that object. A lady's waist looked very small in comparison with the large sleeves and the full skirt. This was called the hour glass figure.

Bicycles became popular during this era and women began wearing a type of bloomer to allow easy movement of her legs without fear of the skirt become tangled in the wheel. (See picture on next page.)

Every woman owned a tailored suit. There is a beautiful sample of this practical and lovely outfit on the next page.

Dress with puffed sleeves from 1895

In the book *Etiquette for Americans* published in 1898, we find this description of dress.

Most women prefer to be dressed in dark clothes for shopping and crowds, and sometimes carry this careful doctrine to the extreme of making themselves uncomfortable. In these days of extremely light clothes, and washable attire for summer, it is more economical to dress in cotton gowns—or shirts and dark skirts, and as so many do it, it no longer makes one conspicuous.

Coats 1893

Victorian 1890s   59

Godey's Magazine discusses what kind of fabric would be used during the summer of 1894.

Lawns and organdies will be greatly used this summer. They are not expensive, ranging in price from twenty-five up to seventy-five cents per yard. When simply made they are easily washed and always look fresh and bright. When trimmed with strips of ribbon they are easily taken out and replaced after the gown has been washed.

A curious combination of colors that enters largely into summer gowns is blue and green. As green is a composite color, and indebted to a mixture of blue and yellow for its existence, the shade chosen to go with blue must be pale and delicate. A bright grass green combined with turquoise blue is hideous, nor do I think that the union is ever very harmonious.

Bicycling outfit 1895

Ladies skating outfit 1897

The *Godey's Magazine* of 1895 has this to say about how women of all shapes have been considered in the fashions.

In fact, the designers have been sufficiently considerate to create styles to suit everybody. Nowadays if a woman is badly dressed it is her own fault, and she can ascribe it to no one else.

The variety in fancy fronts, pelerines [a small cape with long ends in front], and boleros [a short jacket that is open in the front] make it possible for a woman who possesses one good black shirtwaist, even though a little worn, to appear as if she owned a number. Square yokes of tucked chiffon are edged with filmy velvet-trimmed frills, and a fluffy arrangement about the neck. These elaborate little affairs are easily pinned on to a plain shirtwaist.

Velvet is greatly used for dressy carriage and theatre coats. Fur-lined circulars of crimson, gray, or beige cloth are useful and warm for evening; many of them reach well below the waist and frequently to the knees. Long wraps which entirely cover the dress are quite the thing for ball or opera, as they protect the delicate fabric beneath, and are extremely comfortable.

Ladies dress 1895

60 ～ **Costumes with Character**

There is only one quality worse than hardness of heart and that is softness of head. -Theodore Roosevelt

A gracious woman has gracious friendships. -Mary Slessor

Do what you can, with what you have, where you are. -Theodore Roosevelt

Blessed are the single-hearted, for they shall enjoy much peace. If you refuse to be hurried and pressed, if you stay your soul on God, nothing can keep you from that clearness of spirit which is life and peace. In that stillness you will know what His will is. -Amy Carmichael

Victorian 1890s

High Collar Dress

Stand-up Collar
Iron-on interfacing
1"x51" Lace
Fabric same color as the dress

Instructions
1. Use the collar patterns on page 63 as a guide to cut out fabric. Also cut 1" lace 51" long or use gathered lace that is ½" smaller than the length of the collar
2. If using gathered lace, skip this step. Gather the 1"x51" lace to the same length as the collar. Hem each end of the lace with a ¼" hem.
3. Iron the interfacing to the wrong side of one of the collar pieces. Pin the lace on top of collar (FIG. 1). With right sides together, sew three sides of the collar together, using ¼" seam allowance (FIG. 2). Clip corners and turn right side out.

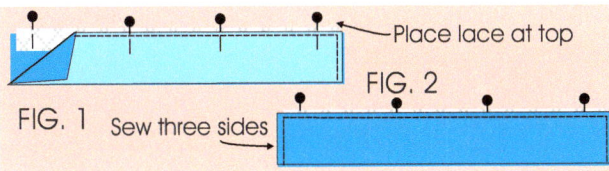

4. Press the outside edge of the facing piece under ¼" (FIG. 3) and top stitch.

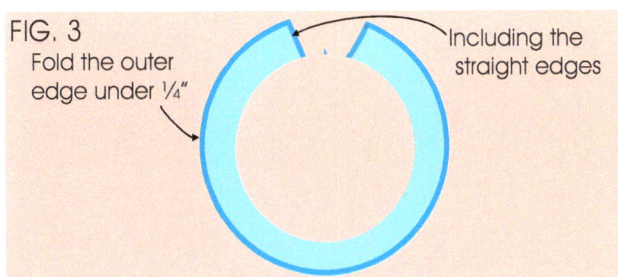

5. With right sides together, sew the raw edge of the collar to the raw edge of the facing piece, using ¼" seam allowance. Pull the facing piece straight to fit the collar (FIG. 4).

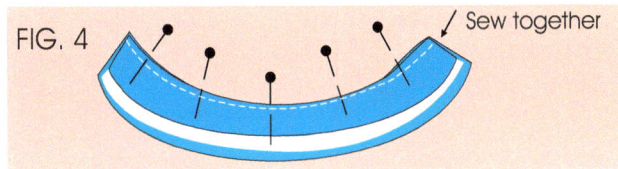

6. Attach hook and eye to close collar.
7. To wear, safety pin facing to the dress facing and close hook and eye.

Hat
Heavy weight fabric
Clothes line wire or millinery wire if available
Iron-on interfacing
½" piece of ¼" tubing

Instructions
1. Use the hat patterns on page 63 as a guide to cut out the hat brim #1, hat brim #2, hat band, and hat top pieces.
2. Iron hat brim interfacing onto the hat brim #2 piece which is larger than the hat brim #1 piece. Then cut the hat brim #2 to the same size as the hat brim #1 and cut the oval out of the center. The fabric shrinks when the interfacing is applied, so cutting the fabric after the interfacing is applied will insure the hat brim pieces are the same size.
3. Iron the interfacing pieces to the hat band and hat top pieces.
4. Take the hat casing piece and press down ¼" on wrong side of the inside circle (FIG. 5). Top stitch around folded edge (FIG. 5).

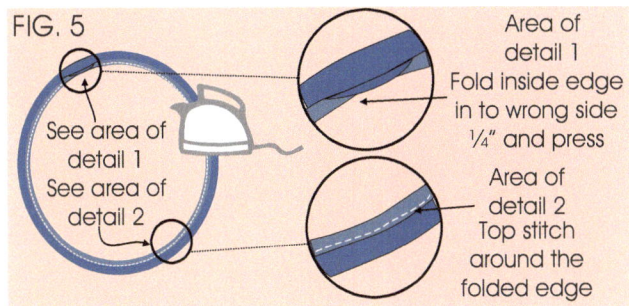

5. Place wrong sides of the hat brim #1 and #2 together, then place the casing on top of the hat brim pieces with the wrong side up. Sew together, using ¼" seam allowance. Cut off excess fabric (FIG. 6).

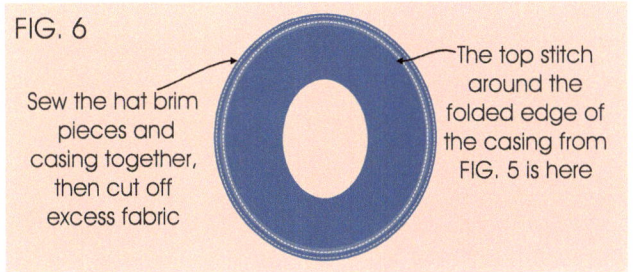

6. Pull the casing over the raw edges and press. Top stitch casing to hat brim, leaving a 2" opening at the back of the hat to thread the wire through (FIG. 7). The side with the casing is the underside.

62   Costumes with Character

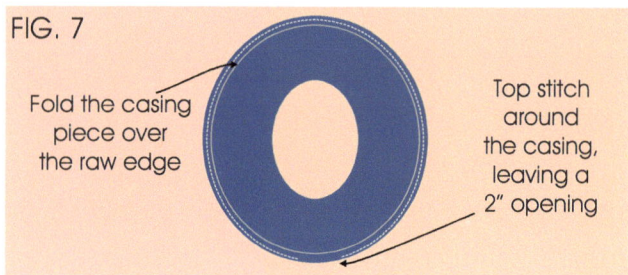

FIG. 7 — Fold the casing piece over the raw edge. Top stitch around the casing, leaving a 2" opening.

7. Sandwich the hole for the head on the hat brim in between the hat band piece and the hat band facing piece. Pin the hat band piece to the top side of the brim hole. Pin the hat band facing piece to the wrong side of the hat brim hole (FIG. 8). Sew the pieces together, leaving about a 2" space between the ends of the hat band piece. Sew the ends of the hat band piece together after the length has been determined and cut off excess fabric. Now sew the remainder of the hat band piece to the hat brim. Fold the facing piece up into the hat band piece, encasing the raw edges, then sew to the hat band piece about ½" from brim. The seam will be hidden by a ribbon when the hat is done.

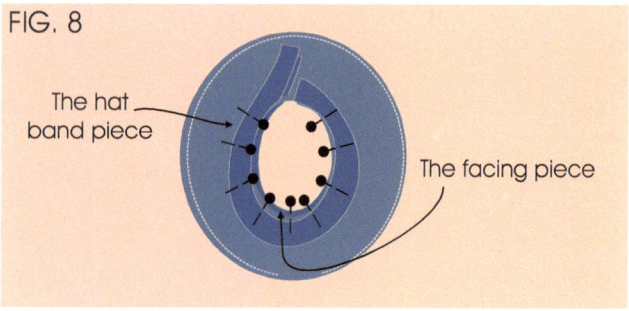

FIG. 8 — The hat band piece. The facing piece.

8. With right sides together, sew the hat top to the hat band (FIG. 9).

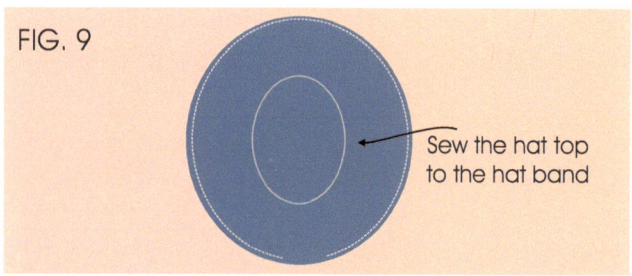

FIG. 9 — Sew the hat top to the hat band

9. Cut a piece of wire that is the same size as the hat brim casing. Push the wire through the casing and connect the ends by placing them into a ½" long by ¼" diameter tube. Hand stitch the casing closed.
10. Tie a ribbon or piece of lace around the hat band. Decorate the hat with silk flowers, feathers, and ribbons. Attach by tacking to the hat with needle and thread, so the hat maybe redecorated easily.

Ruffle Collar - Refer to the Victorian 1880s chapter (page 55).

Handbag - Refer to the Patriot chapter (page 19).

Fan - Refer to the Patriot chapter (page 20).

Belt - Refer to the Sailor chapter (page 50).

Handkerchief at throat - Refer to the Civil War chapter (page 42).

Questions about the 1890s

Answers are below.
1. This American inventor made his first automobile in 1896. What was his name?
2. In what city was the 1893 World's Fair?
3. Name the wives of the three Presidents during the 1890s. Benjamin Harrison, Grover Cleveland, and William McKinley.
4. In what war was the motto "Remember the Maine" used?
5. What was the name of the husband and wife team that discovered radium and polonium in 1898?
6. This silver-tongued orator, who was a devout Christian and fought against evolution years later in the Scopes Trials, ran against McKinley in the 1896 Presidential election. What was his name?

1. Henry Ford 2. Chicago 3. Caroline Lavinia Scott Harrison, Frances Folsom Cleveland, Ida Saxton McKinley 4. The Spanish-American War, 1898. The war was fought between Cuba and Spain, but when the Maine, a U.S. ship, was destroyed the United States became involved. 5. Pierre and Marie Curie 6. William Jennings Bryan

Recommended Resources

Anne of Green Gables & *Anne of Avonlea* by Lucy Maud Montgomery
In His Steps by Charles M. Sheldon
Mary Slessor: Forward into Calabar by Janet Benge
In His Steps by Charles Sheldon
Letters on Practical Subjects to a Daughter by William B. Sprague
Movies - *Anne of Green Gables* (1985) & *Anne of Avonlea* (1986) starring Megan Follows
Movie - *I'd Climb the Highest Mountain* (1951) starring Susan Hayward and William Lundigan
Movie - *The Little Princess* (1939) starring Shirley Temple and Richard Green

 Find recommended resources for the other eras at www.AmyPuetz.com/CWCresources.html

Victorian 1890s Patterns

Stand-up Collar
2½" by the length of the dress neck
cut 2

Hat
Measure size of head and use sizes on next page to determine size to cut for head, then measure 4" out from there.

Stand-up Collar Facing Piece
Use the inside measurement of the dress neckline to determine the size of the facing piece, and make it 3" wide.

Head size ↔ 4"

Hat Brim #1
Cut 1 out of fabric and 1 out of interfacing

Hat Brim #2
cut out an oval that is ½" larger than the Hat Brim #1

Cut an inside opening after the interfacing has been ironed on

Hat Casing
cut the same size as the outside diameter of the hat brim and ½" wide.

Hat Top
about 1" larger than the head size in the hat cut 1 out of fabric and 1 out of interfacing

Hat Band
30"x2½" cut 1 out of fabric & 1 out of interfacing

Hat Band Facing Piece 30"x1"

64 ~ **Costumes with Character**

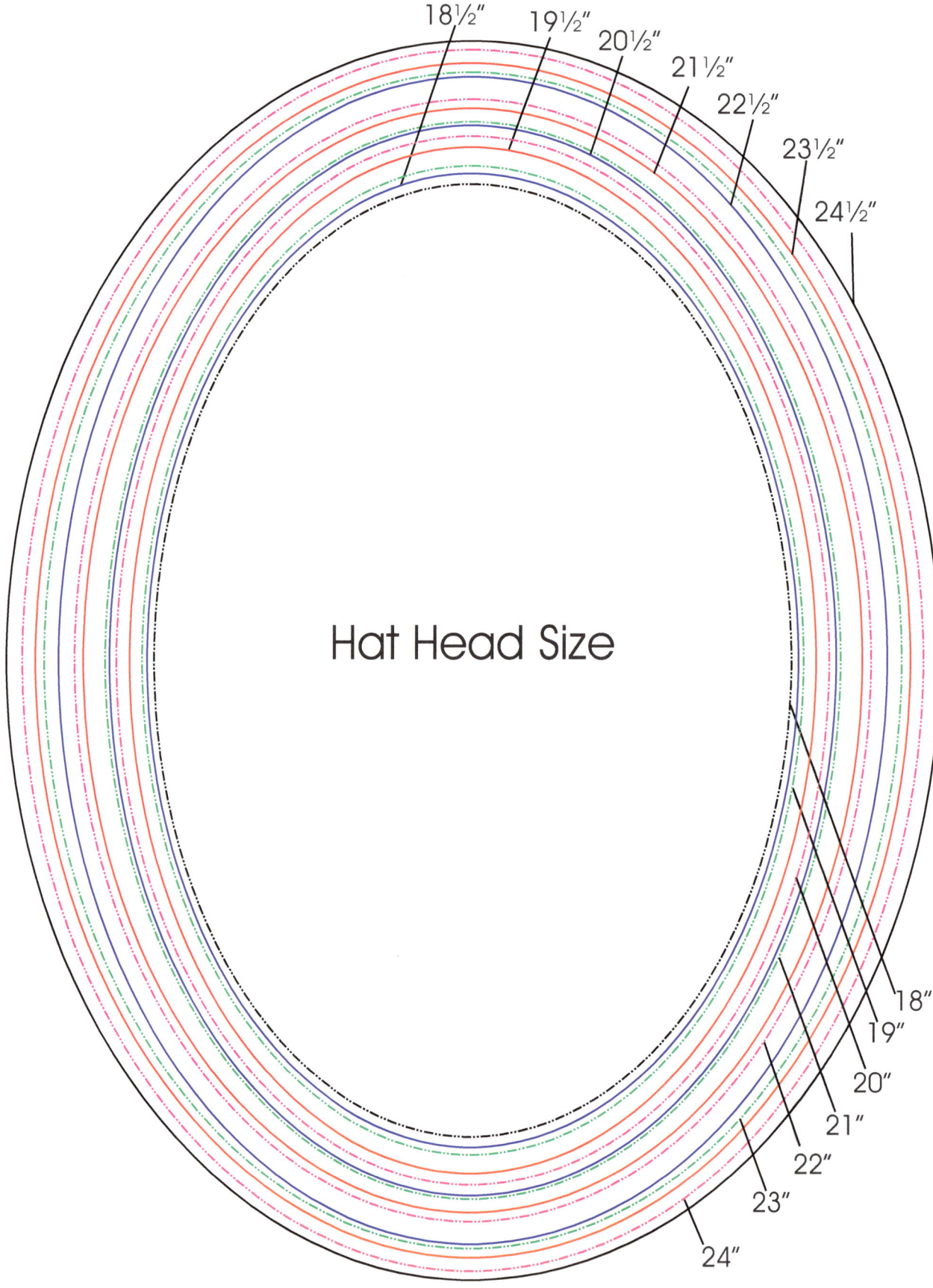

Hat Head Size

Turn of the Century
1900-1910

Things changed drastically during the turn of the century. New inventions like automobiles and airplanes showed the world what American ingenuity could do. The deaths of two national leaders saddened the world. The beloved monarch of England, Queen Victoria, died in 1901. She had ruled for over sixty years. In America President McKinley was assassinated and the hero of the Spanish-American War, Teddy Roosevelt, became the president. His lively family kept the country in fits of laugher with their mischief. One of the boys even brought a pony into a bedroom of the White House!

The fashions of this time were feminine and very pretty. A corset held the ladies in an odd posture with their torso being pushed forward. The puff at the front of the shirts was drawn in by a belt that showed a small waist. High collars were still fashionable except on evening gowns. The puffed sleeves of the 1890s continued for a time but eventually gave way to a straighter sleeve. A little fullness remained just above the cuff [pictured at right and below] and was called a bishop sleeve.

Tailored dresses continued in popularity as the ones on the top of the next page show.

Coats 1902

One of the most noticeable characteristics of this era was the full hair styles. The pompadour, as it was called, was accomplished by pulling the hair over hair pads that were known by the unattractive name of hair rats! The full hair gave rise to large, elaborate hats.

A sample of girls clothing from this era is shown in the photo at left.

In 1905 *The Delineator Magazine* talked about the latest fashion.

A s individualism in matters of dress becomes more pronounced, the boundary lines of fashion grow more and more vague. The French woman breathes in the spirit of the moment's fashion and expresses it in a hundred different versions suited to her particular demands, and the American woman—who was once a slave to Fashion's every whim—has likewise learned to appreciate her own charms

Girls and young ladies outfits from 1902

Costumes with Character

Hats 1902

Ladies suit 1905

and refuses to adopt unquestioningly every vagary in dress. Happily there are becoming styles for everybody in the present-day modes. There are many unusually attractive designs for spring, and chief among them is the shirt-waist dress. Both plain and fancy effects will be worn, the style depending entirely upon the occasion. All sorts of materials will be used to make these smart, practical dresses. For morning wear the silky mohairs in either plain or plaid effects are newest and at the same time most practical, while for the dress that is to have a touch of elaboration there are pretty silks, with taffeta in the lead. There is nothing like a trim, becoming tailor-made suit for all around use. In plain, lightweight cloth, with the skirt just escaping the ground, and jacket with gracefully shaped sleeves large enough to take in the blouse sleeves, such a suit may literally go from the shops to the drawing room musicale. For the morning jaunt a tailored shirt-waist is worn with this costume, and a simple turban and heavy gloves complete the outfit. For afternoon, the same suit is accompanied by a dressy hat, light gloves, and a blouse either of pale-tinted silk or of the lingerie order. There is infinite variety in the spring coat. It ranges from the jaunty, abbreviated bolero [a short jacket that is open in the front] to the graceful, enveloping redingote [a long coat that is open in the front to reveal the dress]. There is still the blouse, which, like the bolero, refuses to die, and which in some of the newest garments preserves more than a suggestion of the pouch. Drape effects characterize the simplest shirtwaists as well as the dressy gowns: but these swathed bodices require skilful adjustment, and a well-fitted lining is essential.

Dresses 1905

Recommended Resources

Rebecca of Sunnybrook Farm by Kate Douglas Wiggins
Mother by Kathleen Norris
Amy Carmichael: Rescuer of Precious Gems by Janet Benge
Helen Keller: From Tragedy to Triumph by Katharine Wilkie
Pollyanna & Pollyanna Grows Up by Eleanor H. Porter
Daughters of Destiny by Noelle Goforth, read the chapters about Queen Victoria and Mary Slessor
Movie - *Pollyanna* (1960) starring Hayley Mills and Jane Wyman
Movie - *The Little Kidnappers* (1990) starring Charlton Heston

Turn of the Century 67

I care not what others think of what I do, But I care very much about what I think of what I do. That is character! -Theodore Roosevelt

God is never behind time. -Mary Slessor

The humblest citizen of all the land; when clad in the armor of a righteous cause; is stronger than all the hosts of error. -William Jennings Bryan

You can give without loving, but you cannot love without giving. -Amy Carmichael

Lady's Cuffs & Vest

Cuffs

Fabric that compliments the dress fabric
Iron-on interfacing
6 Buttons

Instructions (make two)
1. Use the patterns below as a guide to cutting out fabric.
2. Iron interfacing to the wrong side of two of the cuff pieces.
3. With rights sides together, sew each of the cuffs, using ¼" seam allowance and leaving a small opening to turn through (FIG. 1).

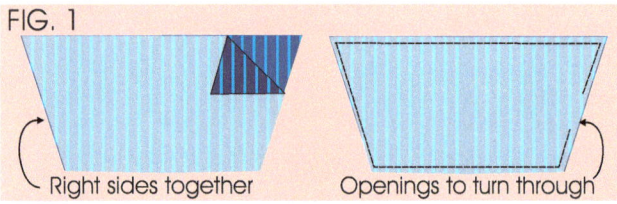

4. Turn right side out and press. Top stitch opening.
5. Make three button holes on each cuff (FIG. 2). Hand sew three buttons on the edge that has the top stitching on it, so when it is buttoned up the top stitching will not be visible.

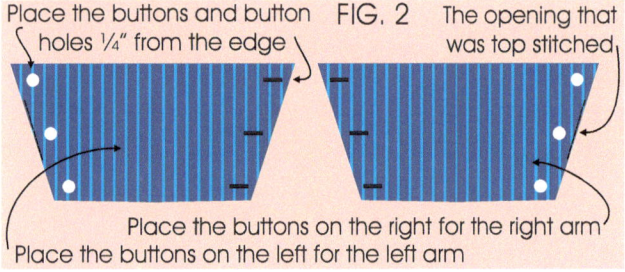

6. To wear, place the cuffs over the dress sleeve and button. The larger part of the cuff goes on the larger part of the arm.

Belt

Fabric that compliments the dress fabric

Instructions
1. Use the instructions on page 69 as a guide to cut out fabric.
2. With right side together, sew belt pieces together in the front.
3. Fold each edge down ¼", then over again ¼" and top stitch.
4. To wear, pin the back together with safety pins or attach Velcro to close the back.

Vest

Fabric
String

Instructions
1. Use the patterns on page 69 as a guide to cut out fabric.
2. With right sides together, sew the front and back together, using ½" seam allowance (FIG. 3).

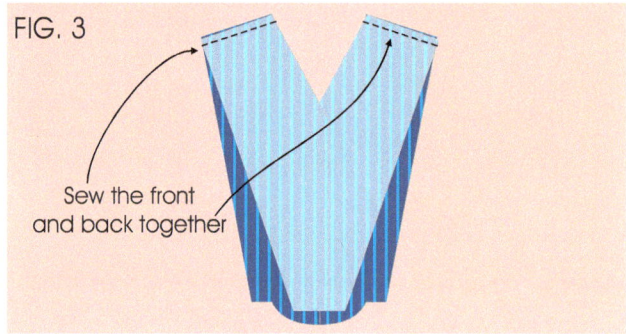

3. With right sides together, sew the facing pieces together.
4. With right sides together, place the facing on vest, lining up seams, the corners in the front, and the V in the back and pin. Sew together, using ¼" seam allowance. Clip fabric at corners and V (FIG. 4).

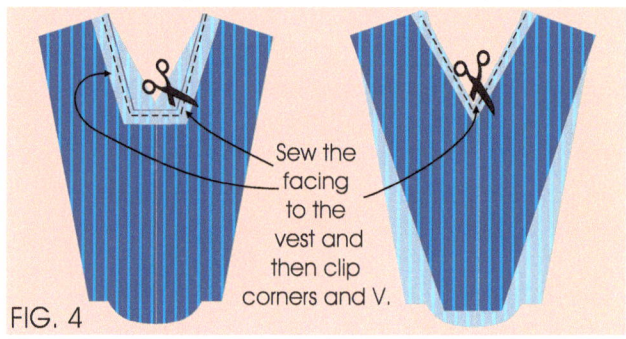

4. Press facing to wrong side ¼" and then over another ½" so the facing is not visible from the front. Top stitch.
5. Press the outside edges of the vest to the wrong side ¼", then over another ¼" and top stitch (FIG. 5).

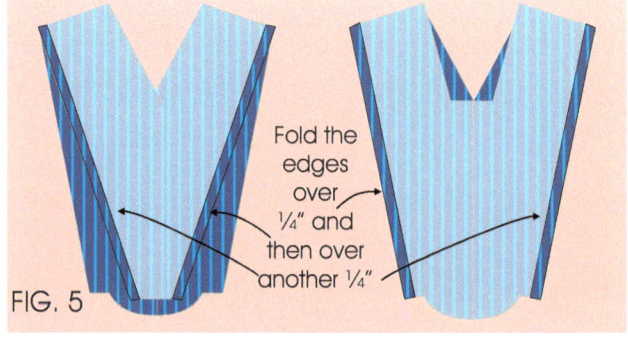

Turn of the Century

6. Gather the front (FIG. 6).

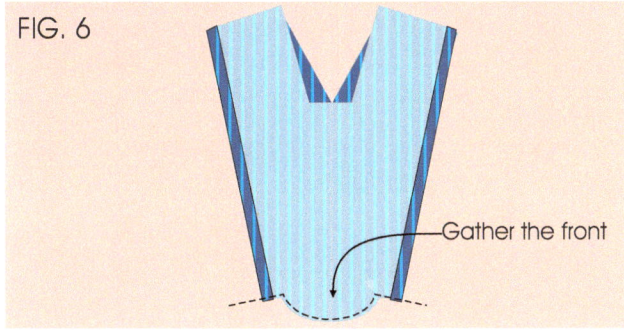
FIG. 6 — Gather the front

7. Turn under 1" for casing. Turn back under to wrong side 1" for casing. Thread a string through the casings in the front, then around through the one in the back so the string ends are together on one side.

8. To wear, place vest over dress bodice and tie string that is through casing at side of waist. The string will help hold the vest in place and will be covered by the belt.

Collar - Refer to the Victorian 1890s chapter (page 61).

Hat - Refer to the Victorian 1890s chapter (page 61).

Handbag - Refer to the American Revolution chapter (page 19).

Questions about the Turn of the Century

Answers are below.

1. Name the president who was assassinated in 1901.
2. This beloved Queen of England died in 1901 after ruling for 64 years. What was her name?
3. Which hero of the Spanish-American War was elected president in 1904? What is the name of the child's toy named after this president?
4. Which lady missionary from Scotland went to Calabar, a region of Nigeria, to spread the gospel? She was called "White Ma" by the natives.
5. Name the brothers that had their first successful flight in 1903 at Kitty Hawk, North Carolina.
6. Who was a well known missionary lady to India? She started Dohnavur Fellowship, a place of safety for temple children.

1. William McKinley 2. Queen Victoria 3. Theodore Roosevelt, Teddy Bear 4. Mary Slessor 5. Orville and Wilbur Wright 6. Amy Carmichael

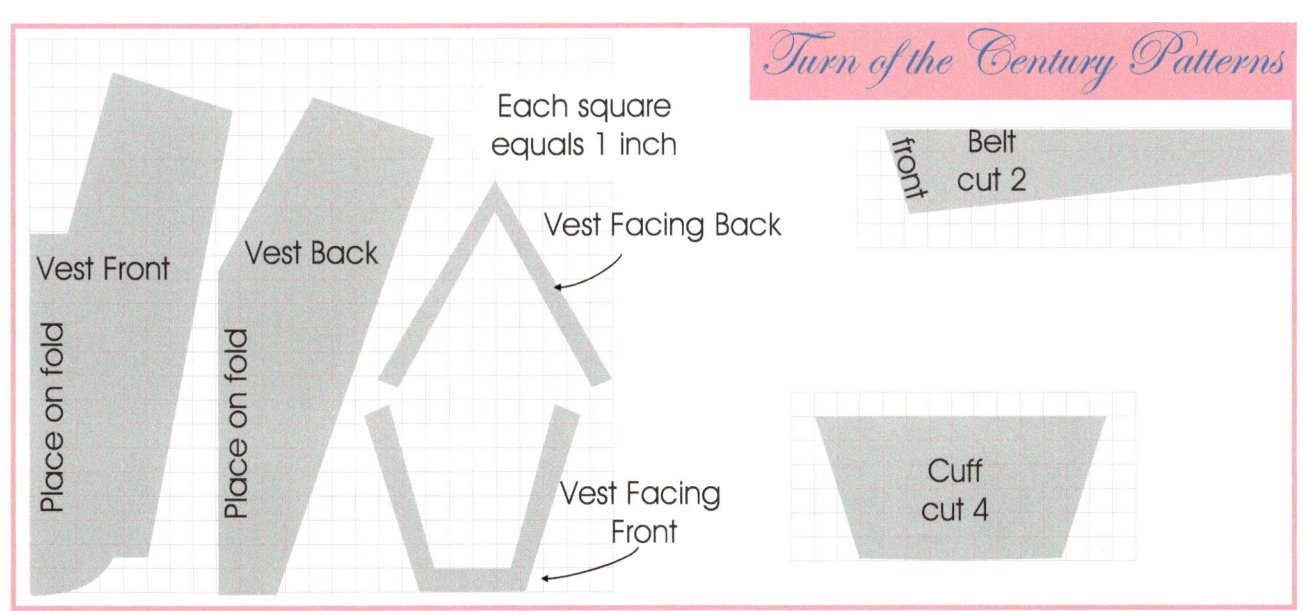

Turn of the Century Patterns — Each square equals 1 inch. Vest Front (Place on fold), Vest Back (Place on fold), Vest Facing Back, Vest Facing Front, Belt front cut 2, Cuff cut 4.

Tea Party
Historical Fun

Tea time was an important part of the Victorian era. Our modern minds associate tea time with people sitting around drinking endless cups of tea and eating dainty cakes. However, in the Victorian era tea time was actually a meal that was eaten about four in the afternoon. The middle class would have eaten it as their last meal of the day while the wealthy would have supper at eight or nine o'clock.

Below we find advice about having an afternoon tea from *Practical Homemaking* by Mabel Hyde Kittredge

The attitude of a girl at meals can make or spoil that meal for the entire family.

Each member of the family should cultivate a habit of appreciation; that is, don't be fault-finding, but take the food that is on the table and eat it with apparent pleasure. There are girls who always come to the table in a fault-finding mood, seeming to take pleasure in saying that they "hate" this or that dish, forgetting that someone has worked hard to prepare it. A bad temper or an unhappy mood while eating is bad for the stomach and often produces indigestion. Talking pleasantly and eating slowly, while at meals, aid digestion.

When a meal is ready, go at once to the table. If you are late, the food gets cold and you have spoiled the pleasure of the cook, as well as annoyed the family and ruined the taste of your own meal. A meal is a family gathering. No one must think of herself alone, but of what will give the entire group the most pleasure. Do not be over-anxious as to what is on your plate. Keep your eyes open. Notice when someone wants their plate replenished or their water glass refilled, or is in need of butter, salt, pepper, or such things.

Method of Making Tea
Never use water that has boiled before or has been standing in the teakettle. Draw fresh cold water and let it boil for the first time. Water that has boiled before and stood on the stove tastes flat because the air has gone out of it.

The amount of tea to be used depends upon the kind of tea used. The saying goes "a teaspoon for each cup and one for the pot," but this is too much tea; usually two teaspoons for four or five persons is enough.

Warm the teapot by rinsing it with hot water. Put tea into the warm teapot and pour in boiling water. Let it stand five minutes and serve. If you wish to use the tea later pour off all liquid from the tea-leaves and heat this liquid when desired. You will, thereby, avoid drawing the poisonous tannic acid from the tea-leaves.

Tea-Tray
On a tea-tray there should be a clean white traycloth, cups and saucers, teaspoons, tea-strainer, napkins, sliced lemon or milk, sugar, bread and butter sandwiches, toast or crackers, and lastly the freshly made tea.

Tea Party

Bring back a special part of the past by hosting a tea party. I enjoyed many tea parties as a young girl and would like to share some ideas with you.

Invitations

- Colored card stock
- Fabric
- Scissors
- Paper-backed fusible web
- Black pen
- Envelopes & stamps
- Copies of teapot & teacup designs (below)

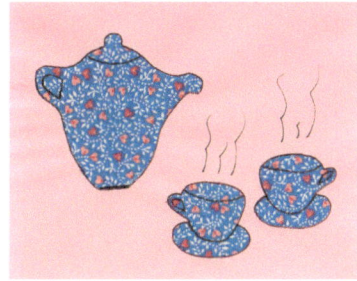

Instructions

1. Iron the fusible web on to the wrong side of fabric.
2. Copy the designs onto a page of card stock and cut the designs out.
3. Trace the designs onto the paper-backed fusible web side of fabric. Cut out the traced designs
4. Cut the 8½x11 card stock in half, making it 5½ by 8½. Fold the card in half, making it 4¼ by 5½.
5. Remove the fusible web paper backing from the cut out teapots and cups. Iron the cut out designs on the folded card stock. Use a black pen to outline the teapot and cups, and make lines of steam.
6. Hand write the information about the tea party on the inside of the card. An example would be:

Miss Eliza Smith (Your Name)
request the pleasure of
Miss Lizzy Miller's (Your Friend's Name)
company at a Tea Party
on June 5, 2011
at two o'clock in the afternoon
123 Your Address

7. Address and mail or personally deliver the invitations.

Games

One of the most exciting things we did at tea parties when I was young was to have a treasure hunt. The treasure may be a teacup and saucer filled with tea bags and tied together with pretty fabric, or homemade dolls, paper dolls, or a pretty doll dress.

For the adventurous girls, you could have a three-legged race or a gunny sack race using large garbage bags in the place of a gunny sack.
Other ideas or games:
~ Musical chairs
~ Button to button
~ Reciting poetry
~ Singing songs
~ Performing a play

Food

There are many things you can make for the tea party. The tea can serve as a light lunch or can be a whole meal or just a morning or afternoon snack. For a light lunch you could serve sandwiches cut in triangle shapes. For a morning or afternoon snack you could serve a cake. Here are some ideas of other things to make:
~ Cream Puffs (my favorite)
~ Petit fours
~ Muffins
~ Scones

The list is endless, so be creative. I am sure you will come up with many great ideas.

Costumes with Character

Index

American Revolution, 15-22
Aprons
    Pilgrim, 8
    Pioneer, 21, 37
Belts
    Civil War, 43
    Sailor, 50
    Turn of the Century, 68
Bonnet (see Hats)
Bustle, 56
Cape, 45
Civil War, 39-45
Collar
    Bertha Collar, 30
    Civil War, 42, 43
    Lace Collar, 55
    Pilgrim, 7
    Puritan, 8
    Quaker, 14
    Sailor, 49
    Square Ruffle Collar, 55
    Stand-up Collar, 61
Colonial, 3-10
Cuffs
    Civil War, 44
    Lace Cuffs, 56
    Pilgrim, 7
    Turn of the Century, 68
Dress, ideas, 1-2
Embroidery Stitches, 31
Fan, 20
Handkerchief, 20, 42,
Handbag, 19
Hats
    American Revolution, 19
    Lawn Cap, 8
    Pilgrim Hat, 7
    Quaker Bonnet, 14
    Romantic Era Bonnet, 32
    Sunbonnet, 37
    Victorian 1890s, 61
    Yachting Cap, 49
Hat Head Size, 64
Hip Pads, 21
Hoop Skirt, 42
Letter Case, 30
Name Cards, 57
Neckerchief, 19
Parasol, 45
Petticoat, 44
Pilgrims, 3-10
Pioneer, 34-38
Pockets
    Civil War, 43
Puritans, 3-10
Quaker, 11-14
Questions, 9, 12, 21, 26, 33, 38, 44, 50, 56, 62, 69
Recommended Resources, 5, 12, 63, 66
Romantic Era, 27-33
Sailor, 46-51
Skirt, 26
Sleeves
    Leg of Mutton Sleeves, 27, 35, 58
    Pagoda, 18
Tea Party, 70-71
Turn of the Century, 65-69
Underskirt, 20, 56
Victorian 1880s, 52-57
Victorian 1890s, 58-64
Vest
    American Revolution, 18
    Turn of the Century, 68
Yachting Cap, 49
Young Republic, 23-26

Bibliography

Blum, Stella. *Victorian Fashions and Costumes from Harper's Bazar - 1867-1898*. Mineola, New York: Dover Publications, Inc., 1974

Clark, Fiona. *Hats: The Costume Accessories Series*. London: B. T. Batsford Ltd., 1982

Darnell, Paula Jean. *Victorian to Vamp: Women's Clothing 1900-1929*. Reno, Nevada: Fabric Fancies, 2000

Ewing, Elizabeth. *Everyday Dress, 1650-1900*. London: B. T. Batsford Ltd., 1984

Foster, Vanda. *Bags and Purses: The Costume Accessories Series*. London: B. T. Batsford Ltd., 1982

Gernsheim, Alison. *Victorian and Edwardian Fashion: a Photographic Survey*. New York: Dover Publication, Inc., 1981

Hill, Margot Hamilton. *The Evolution of Fashion: Pattern and Cut from 1066 to 1930*. New York: Drama Book Publishers, 1983

Holkeboer, Katherine Strand. *Patterns for Theatrical Costumes*. A Spectrum Book, 1984

Lister, Margot. *Costume*. Boston: Plays, INC., 1977

_____. *Costumes of Everyday Life*. Boston: Plays, INC., 1972

McDowell, Bart. *The Revolutionary War*. Washington, D.C.: National Geographic Assistant Editor, 1967

Rogers, Barb. *Instant Period Costumes*. Colorado Springs, CO: Meriwether Publishing Ltd., Publisher, 2001

Thomas, Beverly Jane. *A Practical Approach to Costume Design and Construction Volume I Fundamentals and Design*. Boston, Massachusetts: Allyn and Bacon, Inc., 1982

Tompkins, Julia. *Easy-to-Make Costumes for Stage and School*. Boston: Plays, Inc., 1975

Ulseth, Hazel and Shannon, Helen. *Victorian Fashions Volume I 1880-1890*. Cumberland, Maryland: Hobby House Press, Inc., 1988

Wilcox, R. Turner. *The Mode in Hats and Headdress*. New York and London: Charles Scribner's Sons, 1959

www.ingramcontent.com/pod-product-compliance
Lightning Source LLC
Chambersburg PA
CBHW041159290426
44109CB00002B/64